Lernkrimi Business English

Dirty Business

Woods Delaney

Compact Verlag

Bisher sind in dieser Reihe erschienen:

- Compact Lernkrimi Englisch:
  Grundwortschatz, Aufbauwortschatz, Grammatik, Konversation
- Compact Lernkrimi Englisch GB/US: Grammatik, Konversation
- Compact Lernkrimi Business English: Wortschatz, Konversation
- Compact Lernkrimi Französisch:
  Grundwortschatz, Aufbauwortschatz, Konversation, Grammatik
- Compact Lernkrimi Italienisch:
  Grundwortschatz, Aufbauwortschatz, Konversation, Grammatik
- Compact Lernkrimi Spanisch:
  Grundwortschatz, Aufbauwortschatz, Konversation, Grammatik
- Compact Lernkrimi Deutsch: Grundwortschatz, Grammatik

In der Reihe Schüler-Lernkrimi sind erschienen:

- Compact Schüler-Lernkrimi Englisch
- Compact Schüler-Lernkrimi Französisch
- Compact Schüler-Lernkrimi Spanisch
- Compact Schüler-Lernkrimi Latein
- Compact Schüler-Lernkrimi Deutsch: Grammatik, Aufsatz
- Compact Schüler-Lernkrimi Mathematik

In der Reihe Lernthriller sind erschienen:

- Compact Lernthriller Englisch:
  Grundwortschatz, Aufbauwortschatz, Grammatik, Konversation

In der Reihe Lernstory Mystery sind erschienen:

- Compact Lernstory Mystery Englisch:
  Grundwortschatz, Aufbauwortschatz

Weitere Titel sind in Vorbereitung.

Chefredaktion: Dr. Angela Sendlinger
Redaktion: Paulina Palomino
Fachredaktion: Angela Billington
Produktion: Wolfram Friedrich
Titelillustration: Karl Knospe
Typographischer Entwurf: Maria Seidel
Umschlaggestaltung: Carsten Abelbeck

ISBN-13: 978-3-8174-7658-9
ISBN-10: 3-8174-7658-2
7276581

Besuchen Sie uns im Internet: www.compactverlag.de

Vorwort

Mit dem neuen, spannenden Compact Lernkrimi können Sie Ihre Englischkenntnisse auf schnelle und einfache Weise vertiefen, auffrischen und überprüfen.
Privatdetektiv Kevin Flowers erleichtert das Sprachtraining mit Action und Cleverness. Er und seine fesselnden Ermittlungen stehen im Mittelpunkt einer zusammenhängenden Story.
Der Krimi wird auf jeder Seite durch abwechslungsreiche und kurzweilige Übungen ergänzt, die das Lernen unterhaltsam und spannend machen.
Prüfen Sie Ihr Business English in Lückentexten, Zuordnungs- und Übersetzungsaufgaben, in Buchstabenspielen und Kreuzworträtseln!
Ob im Bus oder in der Bahn, im Wartezimmer, zu Hause oder in der Mittagspause – das Sprachtraining im handlichen Format bietet die ideale Trainingsmöglichkeit für zwischendurch.
Schreiben Sie die Lösungen einfach ins Buch!
Die richtigen Antworten sind in einem eigenen Lösungsteil zusammengefasst.

Und nun kann die Spannung beginnen ...

Viel Spaß und Erfolg!

Inhalt

Lernkrimi 5
Abschlusstest 134
Lösungen 139

Story

Kevin Flowers ist seit sechs Jahren Mitinhaber eines kleinen Detektivbüros in London. Als Spezialisten für Betrug und Wirtschaftskriminalität ermitteln er und sein Kollege David Blood schnell, versiert und erfolgreich.

Dieses Mal werden Flowers und Blood von Preston Stiles, dem Vorstand der Verbraucher- und Umweltschutzorganisation Beyond 2050 angeheuert. Ihr Klient fühlt sich von den Big 3 – den mächtigsten Ölgesellschaften des Landes – bedroht. Scheinbar wollen die Konzerne auf diese Weise die Organisation davon abhalten, weiterhin öffentlich gegen die steigenden Ölpreise zu protestieren. Oder steckt noch mehr dahinter? Haben die Konzerne etwa geheime Preisabsprachen getroffen?
Blood und Flowers beginnen mit ihren Ermittlungen, die sie jedoch in eine ganz andere Richtung führen. Schaffen Sie es, die ganze Wahrheit ans Tageslicht zu bringen?

Chapter 1: A Green Visitor

Spring was in bloom and oil use should have been in decline, yet prices for petrol were continuing to rise. All across London there was a low murmur as every few days drivers had to pay another three or four pence per litre of petrol.
Most people accepted this turn of events stoically, the way they did when waiting in a queue. They looked at the prices, shook their heads and then paid without comment, as if to say: We all have to pay the same prices for petrol, no matter who we are or what profession we practise, whether we have to drive a long way or only round the corner. There's no use complaining about rising petrol prices: you might as well complain about the wind and the rain for all the good it'll do.
After another week, however, a very few voices began to protest. A young woman interviewed for a show called *The Daily Whinge* said, "I don't understand why petrol prices keep going up. Shouldn't someone look into this?"
It did not seem as if anyone in the government thought it was worth investigating. The newspapers, the yellow press especially, can usually be counted on to complain about things such as rising petrol prices, yet they were silent on the issue – more concerned about a football scandal involving betting and an aging football star. Environmental organisations and consumer advocate groups were just beginning to voice concerns.

Übung 1: Übersetzen Sie und enträtseln Sie das Lösungswort!

1. Kommentar ☐ _ _ _ _ _ _
2. Organisation ☐ _ _ _ _ _ _ _ _ _ _ _

3. Untersuchung _ ☐ _ _ _ _ _ _ _ _ _ _ _
4. steigend _ _ ☐ _ _ _
5. üblicherweise _ _ ☐ _ _ _ _
6. Beschwerde _ _ ☐ _ _ _ _ _ _
7. Beruf _ _ _ _ ☐ _ _ _ _ _
8. Preise _ ☐ _ _ _ _

Lösung: _ _ _ _ _ _ _ _

"So, Kevin," David Blood said, "are you going somewhere on holiday soon?"
"If I go anywhere, it will be Ireland."
"What? You're not going somewhere warm? I thought you'd say Spain or Bermuda."
"I just want to go somewhere green," he answered. "The city is so grey and I'm ready for a few other colours, especially green."
A door opened and a chilly breeze gently blew through Blood's thinning blond hair reminding him to put on his hat. It was still early morning, the bells were ringing half-past eight, and the two men were about to leave a café. Kevin Flowers, a year younger than Blood, paid for the coffee and stood.

ÜBUNG 2 !

Übung 2: Setzen Sie folgende Substantive richtig ein!
(Justice, time, clients, office, work, discretion, flight, month, holiday)

"We'd better get to the (1.) ______________," he said, and ran his hand through his brown hair and then checked his chin for whiskers.

"Did you forget to shave?" Blood asked, holding the café door open for people walking in.

"No, I'm just checking to make sure I'm ready to meet (2.) ________________."

"Are we expecting anyone?"

They began to walk towards the office.

"I'm never expecting anyone, but that's usually when someone comes with a sad tale to tell."

"Well, I for one think it's going to be a quiet (3.) ________________, and maybe now would be a good (4.) ________________ for you to get out into nature, Kevin."

"Maybe you should go, Dave. You haven't had a (5.) ____________ since you went to Italy to find the 15-year-old runaway."

"That wasn't a holiday," Blood explained as they turned the corner down a narrow street that led to their office. It was a dark street, even on sunny days, not far from the Courts of (6.) ________________. "That was (7.) ________________, mate."

"You were in Florence. Her parents showed up on a Thursday and you didn't arrive back in London until Sunday night. What were you doing the whole time?"

"That Sunday night (8.) ________________ was the first one I could get, Kev. All the other flights were overbooked."

"That's not what Sally said."

"I need to talk to her about (9.) ________________," Blood said and laughed.

"Sally," he opened the door for Flowers and then followed him into the office, "I thought you weren't going to tell Kevin about Florence."
"Who's Florence, Dave?" Sally Fielding asked, going quickly through the post. A young woman around thirty with thick brown hair, she was the assistant for Blood Flowers Detectives. Since it was a detective bureau, she was more than a secretary: she was office manager and personal assistant, doing whatever needed to be done to help David Blood or Kevin Flowers to recover money or find missing persons, to get to the bottom of whatever case they happened to be working on at the moment.
"Florence, Italy. I'm talking about back in February when I went there to retrieve the runaway."
"I didn't tell him anything," Fielding said, "or if I did it was only to save your life."

ÜBUNG 3 !

Übung 3: Wie lauten die Sätze in der richtigen Reihenfolge?

1. post was Fielding checking Sally the quickly

____

2. was secretary Fielding than a more

____

3. Fielding and manager and assistant office worked personal for as Flowers Blood

____

4. detectives missing retrieve people

____

5. discretion was Sally of absolute Fielding's one qualities

____

"How's your theatre boyfriend doing?" Blood asked, changing the topic. "Still having problems?"

"Not anymore."

"So you've worked things out," Flowers said, "I'm glad to hear that. Too many people don't really try to make a relationship work. They give up the first time there's any difficulty."

"He's turned out to be Mister Wrong," Fielding said without looking up.

"Erm, forget everything I just said," Flowers suggested and walked into his office.

"You don't mean to say you sent him on his way," Blood continued.

"I do," Fielding answered, "but believe me, he's not complaining. You know, he never once gave me roses or tulips or anything of that sort in two years."

Using a voice he thought sounded just the way a grandmother might, Blood said, "you're better off without him, my dear." Putting on a normal voice, he added, "I forgot I have to put something in the post," and quickly ran out of the office.

Not two minutes later the door opened.

"Blood Flowers Detectives?" asked a tall, thin man probably in his early forties.

"Yes," Sally answered, "how may I help you?"
"I'd like to speak to someone about a job."

ÜBUNG 4 !

Übung 4: Welches Wort ist das „schwarze Schaf"? Unterstreichen Sie das nicht in die Reihe passende Wort!

1. work, job, duty, holiday
2. client, patient, customer, consumer
3. company, firm, post, business
4. manager, director, boss, secretary
5. investigate, exercise, research, examine
6. income, charges, costs, expenses

"We're not taking on staff at the moment," she said with a smile.
"I'm talking about giving you or your employers a job."
"Oh, right. That's different."
She walked over to Flowers' office, leaned her head in, and said, "when you get off the phone, there's someone here to speak with you."
A moment later Flowers stepped out of his office and walked up to the stranger with his hand out.
"I'm Kevin Flowers."
"I'm Preston Stiles."
"Nice to meet you. What can I do for you?"
"Do you know who I am?"
"No, should I?"
"I've been on telly often enough."
"I don't have a telly, only a radio."
"So you never even watch football matches?"

"If I want to watch a football match, there's always a pub."
"Have you ever heard of Beyond 2050?"
"It sounds familiar," Flowers answered.
"Well, I'm the director of Beyond 2050."
Just at that moment, Blood walked back into the office.

Übung 5: Sind die folgenden Aussagen korrekt? Markieren Sie mit richtig ✔ oder falsch – !

1. There were heavy protests in London as a result of the rising oil prices. ☐
2. The British media complained a lot about the exploding petrol prices. ☐
3. Consumer advocate groups represent the consumers' interests. ☐
4. Sally Fielding helps Flowers and Blood spend money. ☐
5. Kevin Flowers likes watching TV. ☐
6. Preston Stiles is the secretary of Beyond 2050. ☐

"Do you recognize him?" Flowers asked.
Blood looked at the man carefully, frowning slightly. "I do."
"Well, it's not really about me," Mr Stiles said after a moment.
"No, I do know now. I've seen you on television occasionally."
"I'm director of Beyond 2050."
"Exactly," Blood said, snapping his fingers.
Beyond 2050 were an environmental and consumer advocate organisation, well-known for being outspoken. Their concern for the environment and for people was expressed in their name. In a television interview that had often been replayed, Stiles answered an interviewer as follows:

ÜBUNG 6 !

Übung 6: Unterstreichen Sie die richtige Alternative!

“We’re against everything and anything that’s going to be a blot on the future.”

“What are you *for*?” the (1.) interviewer/writer then asked.

“Well, there are a lot of things that we are *for*, there are so many things that have to be (2.) changed/preserved I’m not sure exactly where to begin – but we are for a clean environment and (3.) investment/involvement in renewable energy sources. We want to see less (4.) responsibility/reliance on animal products because they’re (5.) economical/uneconomical, environmentally harmful and simply unnecessary. We want to see the human race around in another fifty years and are working towards that end.”

“Do you think you’ll be (6.) successful/failing?”

“I am quite (7.) concrete/confident we will be successful.”

“So, what can we do for you?” Flowers asked.

“I came to you because I – or we, rather – have been threatened by some oil companies – the Big 3, they’re called. They have sworn to disrupt our activities and they’ve already begun. They’ve infected our computer network with a new virus, they have somehow managed to have our financial assets frozen – we still don’t know how or why – and they’re beginning to send people to commit crimes in our name – to do things we did not do and then call the police and claim it in our name.”

ÜBUNG 7 !

Übung 7: Übersetzen Sie!

1. Firmen sollten in erneuerbare Energien investieren.

2. Preston Stiles ist Chef einer Umwelt- und Verbraucherschutzorganisation.

____

3. Das Computernetzwerk ist mit einem Virus infiziert.

____

4. Ölfirmen stören die Aktivitäten von Beyond 2050.

____

5. Kriminelle haben die Vermögenswerte eingefroren.

____

"What have they done?" Blood asked.
"They hung a banner from their own refinery with our name on it and a message: 'Leave the North Sea.' But we didn't put the banner there."
"That's hard to prove."
"Scotland Yard does not believe us and you may not either, but that doesn't matter. We're going to pay you to convince yourself that they are doing this."
"Before we agree," Flowers said, "you need to do a little convincing now." As an ex-bobby, Flowers was used to being more direct than diplomatic.
"We have had some direct contact with representatives of the Big 3 and they've threatened us."
"Were there any witnesses?"
The man shrugged his shoulders. "I don't think so. They telephoned me – there couldn't be any witnesses."
"What else?"

"You've noticed the rise in petrol prices?"
"One would have to be blind not to."
"It's starting to get into the news because we have finally made it an issue. We were the first to say that there's something not quite right going on here: the price of oil has gone up but not enough to justify these prices – there are no new taxes and yet prices have skyrocketed. That's when the threats began. Moreover, I have some inside information that some of the local refineries have agreed with the other companies to raise their prices – they've been working together for some time now."

ÜBUNG 8 !

Übung 8: Übersetzen Sie die englischen Sätze und Ausdrücke ins Deutsche!

1. Prices are skyrocketing.

____

2. to do a little convincing

____

3. to get into the news

____

4. to make it an issue

____

5. an agreement between companies

____

6. That is hard to prove.

____

7. to commit a crime

"Who?" Blood asked.
"The Big 3. You know: Golden Day, First Sea Oil and P-Ride."
"Those three companies alone own about 70 percent of the petrol stations around London," Flowers added.
"And about 60 percent around England, Scotland and Wales," Stiles continued. "There was a meeting two days ago between the Big 3."
"Which is not exactly illegal but very suspicious indeed," Blood said.
"The legality depends solely on what they were talking about," Stiles explained. "But they don't want anyone to know about the meeting."
"Do you know who was there or what they were talking about?"
"No," Stiles admitted. "But there's bound to be meeting minutes. And anyway, there's no smoke without fire. They're meeting and prices are going up without any external cause." Stiles looked at the two detectives. "So, what do you think?"
Flowers and Blood looked at each other and Flowers shrugged his shoulders.
"He's a vegetarian," Blood said, by way of explanation, "so he's already on your side."

Übung 9: Finden Sie die Synonyme!

ÜBUNG 9 !

1. company	☐ appointment
2. economical	☐ flourishing
3. successful	☐ to explode
4. director	☐ to accept
5. price	☐ authorised

6. to skyrocket	☐ efficient
7. meeting	☐ firm
8. legal	☐ executive
9. to agree with	☐ fee

"I'm sure you've got connections," Stiles said, "connections even inside Scotland Yard. Keep them informed of what you're doing but under no circumstances mention our name. We don't want to become more of a target for Scotland Yard or for the Big 3 than we already are."

"As long as we feel it's justified," Flowers agreed, "we'll do it your way. How about our fees? It might be a good cause, but much as we might like to we cannot do charity work, you know."

"We're ready to pay your fees and more, if you can prove that the Big 3 have created a monopoly and started harassing us."

They discussed the fees briefly and then Flowers concluded, "we need 30 percent up front, another 20 percent in two weeks and the balance when we have finished."

"Contingent upon results," Stiles said.

"Even if they're results you don't particularly hope for," Flowers added. "Agreed."

They signed an agreement and then exchanged business cards and mobile numbers.

"So," Blood said when Stiles was gone, "you were right this morning. No holiday in Ireland for you, mate."

"I didn't have anything like this in mind, though. A case like this is more complicated than I'd hoped. I much prefer runaway teenagers or finding fathers who aren't paying child support. That's easy in comparison."

"If you're good at it," Blood smiled.

"I'm just pulling your leg," Flowers grinned.

Übung 10: Finden Sie die englische Entsprechung der folgenden Wörter und unterstreichen Sie diese!
(Filiale, Aufsichtsrat, Strategien, Ölpreise, Mitbewerber, Aktionsplan, Gesellschaften, Geschäftsführer, leitende Mitarbeiter, Steuererhöhungen, Preise, Sitzung)

"Where do we begin?"
"Well, Stiles said that First Sea Oil hosted the meeting, so that seems to be the place to begin."
They discussed strategies and next steps and put together an action plan. The first thing to do, they decided, was a bit of research on the companies, names of the CEOs, members of the boards of directors, senior managers. They went through lists of subsidiaries as well as competitors. They looked at oil prices, checked for recent tax increases that hadn't made the news and compared weather in the current spring to the spring of the year before and the year before that. Prices at the stations owned by the Big 3 were increasing substantially but so were the ones at the stations they didn't own.

It did not make sense, so many people simply tried not to think about it. Why worry about something as complicated as all that? The government will take care of us or some consumer organisation will help us out. Something will work out, seemed to be the sentiment.

Übung 11: Übersetzen Sie die Wörter in Klammern und vervollständigen Sie den Text!

"Could be opportunism," Blood theorised. "'Everyone else is (1. erhöhen) ________________ prices, why don't we?'"

"An upward spiral."

"There'll have to be a (2. abwärts) _______________ trend at some point."

"Are you sure you're not just being optimistic, Dave?"

"Right, so our (3. nächster Schritt) _______________ is to visit First Sea Oil. Do you want to go or should I?"

"I'll go. I think it's time for Solicitor Leonard Lawson to (4. überbringen) _______________ some more bad news."

"Another surprise divorce letter?" Blood laughed.

"Just so."

The letter, which was indeed a notification of divorce, looked quite real. The only thing that showed that it was a (5. Fälschung) _______________ was that Flowers and Blood always slightly misspelled the woman's name. They made it subtle enough, however, so that it would not likely be noticed on the first read-through, even by the person addressed in the letter.

Flowers had a real driving license, (6. Kreditkarten) _______________ and (7. Visitenkarten) _______________ bearing the name Leonard Lawson, and he had (8. erfolgreich) _______________ used this second identity a number of times. He usually took the (9. Fälle) _________________________ where going undercover was required, while Blood handled the ones that necessitated finding missing persons. Both agreed it was a (10. gerecht) _______ _________ division of (11. Arbeit) _______________ and that the two ex-bobbies made a good team.

Chapter 2: Paying A Visit

Once the background work on the Big 3 had been completed, the divorce letter was written and a detailed plan of how to get into Mr Pomeroy's office was developed. They also planned what Flowers would do once he was in the CEO's office, should he be lucky enough to get inside. Nothing ever goes quite as designed, they knew, so they always developed a Plan A and a Plan B. Finally, Flowers put on his most conservative black suit, with a white shirt and a dark grey tie.

As planned, he arrived at a time when he could be almost certain of finding the CEO out – just before lunch time. Carrying a black briefcase, he walked slowly up to the reception area, a smile painted on his face, looking as if he were a frequent visitor to the company.

The lobby was large and open with a glass ceiling that revealed the blue sky. Letters – a large red "O" with a blue "N" on the left and a white "S" on the right – hung overhead. Oil is the centre of it all, Flowers thought, as he walked up to the security desk.

"What can I do for you?" asked a young woman wearing a light blue shirt and darker blue trousers which matched those of her colleague, a young man.

Übung 12: Welche deutsche Wendung gibt die Bedeutung des englischen Ausdrucks wieder?

1. fair division of labour
   a) ☐ gerechte Arbeitsteilung
   b) ☐ gute Arbeitseinteilung

2. Nothing ever goes quite as planned.
   a) ☐ Unverhofft kommt oft.
   b) ☐ Nichts ist wie es scheint.

3. A smile is painted on his face.
   a) ☐ Ein Lächeln ziert sein Gesicht.
   b) ☐ Sein Gesicht war geschminkt.

4. That's the centre of it all.
   a) ☐ Das ist das Zentrum der Macht.
   b) ☐ Darum dreht sich alles.

5. to deliver bad news
   a) ☐ schlechte Ergebnisse liefern
   b) ☐ schlechte Nachrichten überbringen

"My name is Leonard Lawson and I have a letter to deliver to Mr Jack Pomeroy," Flowers held up an official-looking letter. The envelope contained a black and yellow design printed in the place for the return address.
"We can take it."
"I'm afraid you cannot simply take it," Flowers said, pulling it back quickly. "It's a legal document which has to be signed for by Mr Pomeroy." Flowers held out the form that required a signature. Like

the driving license, it looked real because it was real.
“We cannot allow you in,” the young man said, stepping in for his colleague.

Übung 13: Welche Präpositionen gehören in die Lücken?
(about 3x, for 2x, to, up 2x, in, of 2x, into)

“That may be,” Flowers replied, “but this is a *legal* document that he has to sign (1.) ________. If you want to run it (2.) ________ to him right now, you can do so but you cannot give it (3.) ________ him without getting his signature first – and you have to be firm (4.) ________ this, otherwise *you* will be (5.) ________ trouble. Do you want to know what’s in this letter? I’ll tell you,” he continued without waiting (6.) ________ an answer, “his wife, Mrs Christine “Christy” Pomeroy, wants a divorce, a quick one. This may come as something of a surprise for Mr Pomeroy, I’m afraid. And it’s going to be an expensive surprise, I can tell you. If one or both (7.) ________ you would like to deliver the letter, here it is. Naturally he’ll ask you what it’s all (8.) ________ . You can say, ‘I don’t know,’ but when he sees your face he’ll know you know and every time he passes you on the way (9.) ________ the office he’ll know that you know something private (10). ________ him. Why don’t you just let me deliver it to him? I’m used to being the bearer (11). ________ bad news. I go (12). _______________ in the lift, deliver it, get the signature and come right back down before you can say 'Bob's your uncle.'"

"What do you think?" the young man asked his colleague.
"I don't know, what do you think?" She looked at her colleague and added in a whisper, "I don't want to deliver that sort of letter."
"Could I see some identification?" The young man asked.
Flowers pulled out a driving license and a business card. The young man studied them a moment and then wrote out a visitor's pass for Leonard Lawson.
"Mr Pomeroy's on the eighteenth floor, sir," the young man said, handing the pass to Flowers.
"I'll be back directly," Flowers said and walked to the lift. He pressed the button for the floor below Pomeroy's. Once the doors closed, he pulled out his mobile phone and dialled.

ÜBUNG 14 !

Übung 14: Übersetzen Sie!

1. Er will einen Brief für Mr. Pomeroy abgeben.

____

2. Der Brief sah sehr offiziell aus.

____

3. Das amtliche Schreiben muss von Mr. Pomeroy persönlich unterschrieben werden.

____

4. Er wählte Mr. Pomeroys Nummer auf seinem Handy.

____

5. Können Sie sich ausweisen?

____

"First Sea Oil, extension please." "I'd like to speak to Ms Margaret Sullivan, please." She was Mr Pomeroy's personal assistant.
"I'll put you through."
"Thank you."
"Margaret Sullivan, Mr Pomeroy's office."
"Purchasing Department here," Flowers said, putting on a strong accent which he called his 'happy idiot accent.' "We have the new armchair Mr Pomeroy ordered."
"Mr Pomeroy did not order a new armchair," she responded rather arrogantly.
"Says here he did, ma'am, and we have it for him."
"Just send it over then," she said.
"Can't do that, ma'am."
"But you're in another building. I am not going to walk all the way over to you and carry it back myself."
"Just a spot of exercise, ma'am. Besides, you don't have to carry it back."
"I'm quite busy at the moment. Why can't you just send it over?"
"You have to confirm that it's the chair he ordered first."
"How can I confirm that it's the right chair," she asked, frustrated, "when I didn't even know he ordered one?"
"Can't help you there, ma'am, but I see your point. I reckon you know him well enough to know if he'll like it, right? It's a question of taste and all that?"

Übung 15: Vervollständigen Sie die Sätze!

1. Margaret Sullivan is Mr. Pomeroy's _____________.
2. A _____________ is an office that buys goods and supplies for a company.
3. A piece of identification that allows someone from outside the firm to enter a business building is called a _____________.
4. Every order has to be _____________ by Ms Sullivan.
5. People who work together in a company are _____________.
6. Flowers had to show his visitor's pass to the _____________ staff.

There was a moment of silence and then Sullivan said, "Right. Okay, I'll be over in a few minutes."
She hung up without saying "goodbye." That was easier than I expected, Flowers thought, and the lift doors opened at the seventeenth floor. He stepped out and looked left and right, frowning, looking confused, a lost puppy, but no one came up to help him. He wanted to give the personal assistant enough time to leave. While monitoring the progress of the three lifts, he looked at his watch and counted off three minutes. One of the lifts stopped at the eighteenth floor and so Flowers took the stairs. He entered the dark stairway and climbed the stairs three at a time and then slowly opened the door to the eighteenth floor. From the doorway, he watched a woman in a black business suit walk into a lift and thought that it must be Margaret Sullivan. I hope it is, he said to himself. He then walked stealthily to the office of the CEO. As he had hoped, there

was no one seated at the desk. He raced past the desk and into the large office that housed Mr Pomeroy's desk. While putting on rubber surgical gloves, he glanced out the large windows which looked out onto London.

Flowers quickly noticed that although the day had seemed clear and beautiful from the ground, it was a hazy, even a dirty day from the eighteenth floor. What a way to see the world, he muttered to himself, and then walked around behind the desk and looked for the calendar.

Übung 16: Finden Sie die englische Entsprechung der folgenden Wörter und unterstreichen Sie diese!
(Aktentasche, Schreibtisch, Führungsstab, Datum, elektronischer Terminplaner, zurückrollen, Tischkalender, Sitzung, Generaldirektor)

ÜBUNG 16 !

He found a desk diary opened to today's date. Flowers paged back to the date of the Big 3 meeting, according to Stiles, and found the afternoon blocked off – but without any explanation. He looked at notes on the desk but saw nothing with the names of the top management of the Big 3 members on it. On the floor next to the desk he saw Pomeroy's briefcase.

Flowers opened it and found the electronic organiser in a pocket. It was already on, so he scrolled back to the date of the meeting. Here was a list of four people who attended the meeting:

CEO of Golden Day James Burnett, P-Ride CEO Archibald Henley and then two people who were in senior management – Alexander Blackbourn (GD) and Julian Rath (P-Ride). There was no mention of who represented First Sea Oil and nothing was included about the content of the meeting, however.

"Stiles seems to have been right," Flowers said to himself. "The meeting took place." Flowers put his hand on the computer mouse and moved it back and forth a couple times. The computer immediately came on. Yes! Flowers thought. He looked at the files most recently accessed but found nothing interesting. He tried to find his way through the computer but the directories were not labelled to be easy to understand, at least not for an outsider, and the files – like the directories – had nondescript titles like LT845. Without being requested to type in a password, Flowers got onto the email account, to look at old emails. Unfortunately, a quick look through the subject lines came up with no "meeting minutes" or anything similar. Flowers pulled out a USB stick, attached it to the computer and copied several directories with their contents onto it. I'm running out of time, he thought and pulled the USB stick out. With a right-click on the mouse, he put the computer back on stand-by. He was walking past the administrative assistant's desk, when she walked back in.

ÜBUNG 17 !

Übung 17: Finden Sie die englische Übersetzung für die Computerfachausdrücke!

1. Maus ____________________
2. E-Mail-Konto ____________________
3. Passwort ____________________
4. Betreffzeile ____________________
5. USB-Speicherstift ____________________
6. Datei ____________________
7. Verzeichnis ____________________

"Who are you and what are you doing here?" she asked.
"I'm Leonard Lawson and I have something very important for Mr Jack Pomeroy," he said, pulling the letter out from the inside pocket of his suit jacket.
"How long have you been here?" she asked.
"Two minutes. Maybe three. Long enough to become impatient and see if Mr Pomeroy was in his office."
She walked into Pomeroy's office for a moment and then walked back out and stared at Flowers suspiciously, her arms crossed on her chest. She then took a quick look at the letter in his outstretched hand.

Übung 18: Bilden Sie zu den Wörtern die entsprechenden Verben mit „to“!

1. receipt ______________________
2. signature ______________________
3. page ______________________
4. notice ______________________
5. explanation ______________________
6. accessible ______________________
7. suspicion ______________________
8. copy ______________________

"Since he isn't here, I need your signature," Flowers said, opening his briefcase and handing her the piece of paper.
"What is this?"

"A legal document."

She looked up at him and made a face that said: I can see that for myself. "That's bloody obvious. What am I signing for?" she asked, frustrated.

"Receipt of this letter. You can sign for Mr Pomeroy, can't you?"

"Of course," she said and shook her head as if to say, 'What a stupid question'.

"I'll find my way out," he said, putting the signed form back into his briefcase, but there was no need to say anything further. Ms Sullivan was taking no further notice of him.

! ÜBUNG 19

Übung 19: Setzen Sie die englische Übersetzung der Wörter in Klammern ein!

(dringend, Büro, unterschreiben, Empfang, persönliche Assistentin, Besucherausweis, Tresen, Schriftstück, Aktentasche)

At the (1.) ________________, the young woman said, "I thought you said you were going to be right back."

"I thought someone would be in the (2.) ________________ who could (3.) ________________ for Mr Pomeroy's mail. I had to wait while someone fetched his (4.) ______________________. She was off on some (5.) _____________ errand."

The young woman held out her hand for the (6.) ______________.

"Can I see the (7.) ________________ you were to have signed?" she asked, once the pass was in her hand.

"You're quite thorough." Flowers raised his eyebrows, then took the form out of his briefcase and laid it down on the (8.) ___________ in front of her. "But then so am I. See? Everything right as rain."

She read the document carefully and then frowned at him, clearly showing her distrust.

Flowers put the document back into his (9.) ______________ and closed it with a snap. "You're definitely in the right line of work," he said and gave her a friendly wave.

"Hello Mr Lawson," Sally Fielding said as Flowers walked into the office.

"It's the suit, isn't it?" Flowers smiled.

"You smell, Kevin!" she said as he stood next to her and began waving her hand in front of her face.

"Sorry, Sal. I got a bit nervous while I was going through the CEO's desk and computer."

"So how did it go?" Blood asked, rushing out of his office.

"Brilliant. Or, better than I expected, in any case. You'll be glad to know that my social engineering skills have not failed me yet."

"No one wants to deliver that bloody letter," Blood laughed.

"Solicitors will do anything," Fielding said with disgust, "even phoney ones."

"You're not serious, are you, Ms Fielding?" Flowers gave her a worried look.

"Yes I am, if you want to know. Mind you, I understand you have to do what you have to do. But people are always abusing trust these days. You're manipulating people, they're manipulating people, everyone is manipulating and being manipulated – no one can trust anyone to be what they say they are today."

"You're thinking about your boyfriend," Blood said, trying to comfort her.

"Maybe, but it isn't just him."

"Things were not better in the past," Flowers said. "The world's always been a bit mad."

"Is that supposed to cheer me up?" Fielding asked, "because if it is, it did not work."

! ÜBUNG 20

Übung 20: Bringen Sie die Wörter in die richtige Reihenfolge!

1. and was Flowers desk computer examining CEO's the

___

2. the needed administrative detective signature the assistant's

___

3. legal handed the her document Flowers

___

4. put form briefcase Flowers back his in signed the

___

5. member is a the of legal solicitor profession a

___

"Come into my office," Blood said to Flowers, and they walked away from Fielding. "She's not taking it so well, I reckon," he added once the door was closed, "you know, two years together and all that."

"We all have to adjust to new situations," Flowers replied.

"So what did you find out?" Blood asked.
"There does appear to have been a meeting. Stiles wasn't pulling my leg – or our legs. I was able to find Pomeroy's electronic organiser and got the names of those who attended. I'm afraid I was not so lucky with finding out what they discussed there, though."
"Yes, but they shouldn't even be meeting in secret," Blood said.
"No, they shouldn't. It doesn't look good. But finding the meeting minutes would have been a nice coup. As it was, I had about ten minutes and I did as much as I could in that time. I got on his computer but he has some complicated system for organising his documents and I couldn't make head or tail of it. Otherwise, everything went as planned."
"What's the next step?"

Übung 21: Übersetzen Sie und enträtseln Sie das Lösungswort!

! ÜBUNG 21

1. Dokument _ _ _ _ □ _ _ _
2. teilnehmen □ _ _ _ _ _
3. Sitzung _ _ _ _ _ □ _
4. manipulieren _ □ _ _ _ _ _ _ _ _
5. organisieren _ _ □ _ _ _ _ _
6. Protokoll _ _ _ _ _ □ _
7. Empfangsbestätigung □ _ _ _ _ _ _
8. System _ _ □ _ _ _

Lösung: _ _ _ _ _ _ _ _

"I don't know. What do you think? Should we try to get into one of the other companies and see if they have any records that would be of interest?"

"What other options do we have?"
"We could just directly approach one of the senior managers who attended the meeting," Flowers suggested, "and put some pressure on him."
"Do you think that would work?" Blood asked doubtfully.
"Senior executives are often the ones who go to prison when things go wrong. They do the dirty work."
"They're just following orders," Blood said, "and they go to jail, while the ones who are pulling the strings get away."
"It's difficult to prove sometimes."
"Everything is difficult to prove."
"That, Davy, is why people need us," Flowers smiled.
"So, what do you think we should do next?" Blood looked his partner in the eyes.
"I could do with a pint."
"Later, Kev. The pubs are closing soon anyway."
"I don't know what the next step is. I'm still thinking about it. I almost forgot," Flowers said and started reaching around his suit looking for a pocket. Finally he found what he was looking for and held up the USB stick.
"We might find something on this, though I must say I'm not that hopeful."
"That's not what I think it is, I hope," Blood gave Flowers a worried look. "You didn't take files off his computer."
"I certainly hope not," Flowers answered. "I only wanted to copy them."
"This material is useless to us in court."
"It opens the door, Dave," Flowers paused shortly. "I had to know if Stiles is telling us the truth. You know how paranoid people can be. How many cases have we taken on where there turned out to be nothing happening?"

Übung 22: Welche Verben und Substantive gehören zusammen? Setzen Sie die entsprechenden Ziffern ein!

1. to attend	☐ the strings
2. to follow	☐ a look
3. to pull	☐ a file
4. to take	☐ a meeting
5. to copy	☐ an order
6. to abuse	☐ trust

Blood put the disk into his computer and glanced over the file names.
"This guy must be a mathematician or else he's simply come up with a very complicated organisational system."
"I know. I just selected a few directories at random. I don't know if there's anything of importance for us on it. It might just be a waste of our time."
"I don't know. I don't have anything else to do at the moment, so I'll just look around a bit."

Chapter 3: The Mask Becomes the Man

Flowers went off to research P-Ride a little more, while Blood read through the computer files. A couple of hours later, Blood called for Flowers loudly.
"Kevin, come in here. You've got to see this."
Flowers got off the internet web site he had been reading through and stepped into Blood's office.
"What did you find?"
"Okay, first of all, none of this is really very important, very dam-

aging or top secret. It does not ask for passwords or anything of that sort. Pomeroy's a very trusting bloke, apparently. I can't believe he left his computer on. There must be a password required to get into his files. You must have got there just after he left and the automatic off switch had not done its trick yet."

ÜBUNG 23 !

Übung 23: Welches Wort ist das „schwarze Schaf"? Unterstreichen Sie das nicht in die Reihe passende Wort!

1. examination, check-up, check-in, assessment
2. obviously, apparently, clearly, nearly
3. importance, signature, significance, value
4. computer, complicated, complex, difficult
5. command, instruction, order, arrangement
6. copy, reproduction, research, duplicate
7. material, data, facts, files
8. opportunity, option, alternative, choice
9. understand, make out, ignore, recognize
10. increase, raise, elevate, come upon

"Okay, Dave, I get the idea. Now, what did you find?" Flowers asked impatiently.
"Not the minutes of the meeting."
"So do you want to tell me what you *did* find?"
"Suggestions."
"For instance?"
"Pomeroy suggests that Burnett and Blackbourn put a little pressure on one of the distributors to raise prices. He doesn't say it directly, but that's definitely what he's getting at."
"What does he say?" Flowers asked.

Übung 24: Setzen Sie das passende Substantiv in die Lücken ein!
(profits, distributors, turnover, raise, translate, increases, market, competing, values)

"He says that 'a bit of weight on a few toes might produce movement in (1.) ________________ and reduce precision.' If you (2.) ________________ that, what he is saying is: with a bit of pressure in the right places someone will be forced to (3.) ________________ prices and reduce transparency. Distributors have to go along with these price (4.) ________________, in other words. Let's face it, First Sea or Golden Day or P-Ride cannot simply raise prices. Everyone has to raise prices. The difference is, the Big 3 make (5.) ________________ as do the (6.) ________________, but not the 30 to 40 percent of the (7.) ________________ that are still (8.) ________________ with the Big 3. Their prices go up, (9.) ________________ goes up but their profits remain the same."

"I'm not sure I quite understand what's happening," Flowers said.
"I'm not sure I do, either," Blood admitted.
"I've been looking into P-Ride this afternoon, but perhaps a meeting with Blackbourn might be the more appropriate next step."
"On the other hand, maybe we're going in the wrong direction with this. I think this is leading us astray. What are we doing? What are we supposed to do? I mean, what's our goal?"
"I see what you mean. We have to get back to Stiles and to what he hired us to do."

They looked at each other for a moment and then sat for a while, silent, each lost in thought.

ÜBUNG 25 !

Übung 25: Finden Sie die passenden Synonyme!

1. turnover	☐ merchant
2. distributor	☐ to propose
3. to compete	☐ volume
4. instance	☐ purpose
5. appropriate	☐ example
6. to suggest	☐ to battle
7. goal	☐ suitable

"There's no mention of Beyond 2050 in anything you've read so far?" Flowers asked finally.

"Not yet. I still have a few more directories to go through, however. Who knows what might turn up?"

"Beyond 2050's banner was hanging from a First Sea refinery not too far from here. Perhaps we need to focus more on them."

"But it might just as well have been Golden Day or P-Ride," Blood argued.

"It might have been, but it wasn't," Flowers responded, "and we don't know one way or the other."

"If they're working as closely as Stiles says, then the other two also know that Beyond 2050 didn't put the banner there."

"But we don't know who did, do we? Just because it was put on a First Sea refinery doesn't mean they put it there."

"And where is the banner now?"

"There's something for you, now, Dave. Find out where the banner is and who made it and then you should be able to find out who bought

it. There has to be a paper trail at least at the banner's producer."
"It might not really tell us who ordered the banner, but perhaps we can then be certain who it wasn't."
"That's something."

Übung 26: Wie lauten die Wendungen im Deutschen?

1. You are pulling my leg!
   a) ☐ Du hast mir Steine in den Weg gelegt!
   b) ☐ Du willst mich auf den Arm nehmen!

2. I couldn't make head or tail of it.
   a) ☐ Ich konnte mir keinen Reim darauf machen.
   b) ☐ Ich konnte nichts dagegen tun.

3. Do you think that would work?
   a) ☐ Glaubst du, das könnte funktionieren?
   b) ☐ Könnte das Arbeit bedeuten?

4. They do the dirty work.
   a) ☐ Sie machen schlechte Arbeit.
   b) ☐ Sie machen die Dreckarbeit.

5. I get the idea.
   a) ☐ Ich habe verstanden, worauf du hinaus willst.
   b) ☐ Ich habe die gleiche Idee gehabt wie du.

6. It might be a good moment to give him a heads up.
   a) ☐ Es ist der richtige Moment, um ihn zu informieren.
   b) ☐ Es ist der richtige Moment, um ihm die Meinung zu sagen.

"Should we call Mac?" Mac was their contact at Scotland Yard. His name was actually Jim Ireland, but Blood and Flowers called him 'Mac' because he worked at *Scotland* Yard.
"It might be a good moment to give him a heads up."
"We don't really have much at the moment, but in the past he's complained that we gave him tips too late."
"Mac, this is David Blood, I wanted to let you know about a project we're working on at the moment."
"What's up, Dave?" Mac asked.
"We've been hired by Preston Stiles at Beyond 2050."
"Have you taken up charity work, Blood? I didn't think you and Flowers did anything for free."

ÜBUNG 27 !

Übung 27: Unterstreichen Sie die richtige Alternative!

"We don't. In fact, they're paying us our normal (1.) wages/fees with the promise of a (2.) benefit/bonus if we get the proof he wants."
"Seems they've got some money. I wonder where they get so much money? What're you doing for them?"
"Stiles says that they didn't put the banner up at First Sea."
"Of course they didn't," Mac said ironically.
"Mac," Blood said, "they usually make a big show out of putting banners up in places like that. He admitted that. I think if they did this, they would have done it in broad daylight – not at night. These (3.) environmental/superficial organisations are anything but introverted."
"So, what's (4.) the matter/the point of First Oil putting a banner up on their own refinery?"
"They might be working together with Golden Day and P-Ride to

(5.) lower/raise prices and discredit the environmental organisations – you know, a little bad (6.) publicity/marketing."
"Well, I'll see what I can find out from here, but I'm (7.) lazy/busy at the moment. Keep me (8.) alive/updated."
"Will do."

It was a beautiful morning, the sun blazing down and warming London and its surroundings. For the moment a member of the police once again, Blood drove off to the oil refinery where the Beyond 2050 banner had been hung. He parked his car in the visitor's car park and walked up to the security office. It was clear that the building was prefabricated: the metal stairs up to the office, the walls that could be moved to expand or reduce the size of rooms, windows with metal sills.
"Hello, I'm John Glaser, constabulary's office," he said to a security guard, "and I would like to speak to the plant manager or someone who can tell me something about the banner."
"May I see some identification?" the guard asked. He was in his fifties and his white hair was cut very short. He looked as though he had spent time in the military.
"I'm here on official business," Blood said, handing him his identification.
"I don't want a tour of the plant," Blood added with a half-smile. "I would like to speak to someone who knows something about the banner Beyond 2050 put on the refinery. Someone here must know, right?"
The guard looked at the card and said, "John Glaser."
"That's me."
"I reckon it is. It'll take me a moment to find out who to send you to, sir," the guard answered in a voice that was neither warm nor threatening.

ÜBUNG 28 !

Übung 28: Lesen Sie den vorausgegangenen Textabschnitt nochmals durch und übersetzen Sie die folgenden Aussagen!

1. Blood parkte seinen Wagen auf dem Besucherparkplatz.

____

2. Er ging hinüber zum Wachschutz.

____

3. Das Gebäude war ein typischer Fertigbau.

____

4. Ist es möglich, mit dem Betriebsleiter zu sprechen?

____

5. Ich bin dienstlich hier.

____

In about 15 minutes, the plant assistant manager walked into the security office. He was about Blood's age but seemed a bit more pleasant than the guard.
"I'm Robert Wisacker, assistant plant manager."
"John Glaser, constabulary's office."
Once again Blood showed his identification and explained what he wanted.
"There were no arrests, correct?"
"The banner was hung at night and we noticed it just before dawn, by which time whoever hung it was gone."
"That's unusual."
"Is it? Come this way," the man said, with a Liverpudlian accent. It sounded to Blood as if he were speaking through his nose.

Übung 29: Setzen Sie die englische Übersetzung der Wörter in Klammern ein!
(Angelegenheiten, herstellen, gemeldet, einkaufen, Berichte, Werbespots, liefern, Tankstellen, erwartete)

"I actually (1.) ________________ someone sooner. We (2.) ________________ this several days ago and were answered only with silence from you all. Trespassing and defacing private property. The news crews were here with cameras but not you."

"I know this is important to you, sir, but we have more pressing (3.) ________________ to deal with. I'm searching for the husband of a battered wife, trying to find two runaway children and writing (4.) ________________ on a series of robberies that have targeted small, Indian takeaways. I think you can understand that this doesn't quite get the priority you would like it to."

The man said nothing in answer.

"So, you (5.) ________________ the petrol here that keeps London running?"

"You've seen our (6.) ________________. Yes, we get shipments of crude oil and refine it into petrol. Then we (7.) ________________ it to (8.) ______________________ all over London and in the surrounding areas as well – as far away as Swindon and Oxford. Sometimes the Americans come (9.) ________________ and we sell to them as well."

"Which raises local prices."

"It can, depending on how much they buy and on the current market supply."

"That's not the case at the moment, is it?"

"Not as far as I know, Inspector Glasser?"

"Inspector Glaser," Blood corrected.

He led Blood down one hallway after another until they came to a storage area. Wisacker took out a ring of keys, selected one and opened the door.

"I didn't realise this building was so large," Blood said as he followed Wisacker in.

The banner was in a corner, folded into a large, thick square. Behind it were boxes and drums. Blood stopped and began to look at the boxes.

"The materials contained in these boxes are a trade secret, Inspector. If you want to look inside them you'll need something from a judge."

"That's not necessary," Blood answered.

Blood lifted the folded banner up onto its side. Though it was an obvious strain, Wisacker stood behind him and made no attempt to help. Once it was on its end, Blood could see one end and he then dragged the banner away from the boxes and drums so he could unfold it.

"I hope you're going to fold it back up," Wisacker looked at Blood reproachfully.

"I'm sure you can find someone to do that, Mr Wisacker," Blood replied.

Once it was unfolded to its full length, Blood studied it a moment, then pulled out a camera that printed pictures almost instantly, and took a few pictures of the banner. Afterwards, he flipped it over and began to examine it.

Übung 30: Beantworten Sie die Fragen zum Text!

1. What did Blood find out about Mr. Pomeroy?

____

2. What did Blood want to discover at the First Sea refinery?

____

3. Why do Flowers and Blood call Jim Ireland 'Mac'?

____

4. Who was Constable John Glaser?

____

5. What did Blood discover at First Sea?

____

"What are you doing?" Wisacker asked.
"I'm looking to see if the manufacturer of the sign attached a label to the banner."
"You don't really expect to find one, do you Inspector?" Wisacker asked with some irritation.
"No, Mr Wisacker, I don't," he answered, looking at the man who was standing a short distance away, as if he were ready to leave. "But I'd be a fool not to look." As expected, there was no label. Blood then took out his Swiss Army knife and poked a hole in the banner.
"What are you doing, inspector?" Wisacker asked, as if Blood's action had been in the nature of a crime.
"You didn't plan on using this banner, did you Mr Wisacker?"
Wisacker sighed loudly while Blood cut a square about the size of his hand in the material at one end of the banner.

"What do you need that for?" Wisacker asked, shaking his head.
"We want to find out who produced this banner."
"And that's going to help you?" he asked, almost laughing.
"It might, Mr Wisacker, it might. I should think you would be glad that we are trying all avenues. Perhaps you don't want to know where it came from or perhaps you know exactly where it came from."
"Inspector, we all know quite well who put the banner there. It's written in large letters. Just look at the photograph you took."
"You know it and I know it, but judges need a little bit more. This is just circumstantial evidence, as far as they're concerned."

ÜBUNG 31 !

Übung 31: Unterstreichen Sie die fünf Sätze, die inhaltlich nicht zum Text passen!

Blood looked at his counterpart for a moment before posing a question: "For example, Mr Wisacker, how do you know that Beyond 2050 put the banner there? Perhaps Beyond 2050 *did* put the banner up, or perhaps First Sea Oil did. Maybe they wanted to have a little fun. Maybe they are just trying to discredit Beyond 2050. It would not be the first time a company has tried to make a consumer group or an environmental organisation look bad."
"Who's going to buy that?"
"I don't know. Perhaps I would. I've seen just about everything. I've seen your signature on my business plan. But I must say, regardless, that I do not understand your hostility at all." Blood walked up to Wisacker and stood directly opposite him. "Is there something you're not telling me?"
The two men stared at each other. Then they started a little square dance.

"Are you finished here?" Wisacker asked, finally, breaking the silence.
"Yes, I am, thank you. And I think I'm going to apply for a job at this refinery."
Wisacker led Blood back to Security in silence. "Do you want to see where the banner was hung?" he asked, suddenly becoming a bit more friendly. Wisacker pulled out his electronic organiser.
"It's not absolutely necessary, but if it isn't too much of a problem then why not?"
Blood followed Wisacker outside where he pointed to a tall chimney. "There," he said.
"And how would someone get all the way up there?" Blood asked.
"That's what I'd like to know. There's a team in Security twenty-four hours a day, seven days a week. We have cameras all over, too."
"How many?"
"That's restricted information. I have forgotten the password of my computer."
"Yes, of course."
"You can be sure the crew on duty the night the banner went up were thoroughly questioned. I would have sacked them all, myself, if the decision had been left up to me. But it wasn't."
"Could you give me their names? One day I will be the CEO of one of the three big oil companies!"

Wisacker wrote down several names on a notepad he kept in the inside pocket of his jacket and then handed the sheet to Blood.
"Here, Inspector. I would prefer if you did not question them while they're on duty."
"So, how does someone get in here from outside?"
"Preferably you don't. A tall fence surrounds the entire facility. You would have to climb over the fence which has barbed wire at the

top. And there are a number of places where you would be well lit up at night, especially there where they hung the banner – the whole refinery is lit up at night like a Christmas tree."

"How do you think they got in? Did they make any holes in the fence?"

"We haven't found any damage. They didn't cut any holes into the fence and I really can't imagine they climbed over it, not with the barbed wire and that heavy banner to carry."

"That would be quite a lot to carry," Blood agreed.

"Ladders in the refinery itself are locked, so they couldn't just climb up. I would be interested to know just how they managed it myself, Inspector."

ÜBUNG 32 !

Übung 32: Kreuzen Sie die richtige Übersetzung an!

1. Ich hätte sie alle entlassen!
   a) ☐ I would have sacked them all!
   b) ☐ I would have let them all go!

2. Wer sollte das wohl glauben?
   a) ☐ Who's going to buy that?
   b) ☐ Who's going to think that?

3. Wenn es nicht zu viele Umstände macht.
   a) ☐ If it's not too much circumstantial.
   b) ☐ If it's not too much of a problem.

4. Sie sind gerade alle im Dienst.
   a) ☐ They're all on duty now.
   b) ☐ They're all in the office now.

5. Das würde ich auch gerne wissen!
   a) ☐ You would have to ask me.
   b) ☐ That's what I'd like to know.

6. Er warf ihm einen strafenden Blick zu.
   a) ☐ He gave him a reproachful look.
   b) ☐ He looked at him impatiently.

"In the past, they've made a big production out of putting a banner on an oil refinery, using helicopters and that sort of thing and they do it in broad daylight, expecting to be arrested. Civil disobedience."
"Well, there was no show this time."
"I wonder why."
"You would have to ask them."
"I plan to. Thank you for your time," Blood said and walked away.
When he got to the visitor parking lot, Blood turned around and looked to see if Wisacker was still there, waiting to make sure that Inspector Glaser left, but he was gone. I wonder what was in those boxes, Blood thought, as he backed out of the visitor's car park.
When Blood walked into the office with the fabric, Flowers was not there. "Where's Flowers?" he asked Fielding.
"The news reporter went off to speak to Alexander Blackbourn at Golden Day, I think it is."

Flowers pulled out a cassette player. "Do you mind?" he asked, pulling out a pad of paper at the same time.
"You have ten minutes, Mr Rogers," Alexander Blackbourn said. "I'm a very busy man." He was a heavy-set man, with a red face, and hair on three sides of his head but not on top. The buttons on his white shirt were tight across his rolling belly which strained against the shirt the way an excited dog strains against a leash.

ÜBUNG 33

Übung 33: Finden Sie das passende Gegenteil zu den Ausdrücken in Klammern!

Blackbourn and Flowers were sitting opposite each other (1. behind) ________________ Blackbourn's large oak desk.

"Thank you for your time. I have only a few (2. answers) ________________. First is, can you explain why the price of petrol has been going up and up?"

"The price of oil is quite (3. low) ________________."

"But it isn't going up. It's stayed about the same for the past month."

"Yes, but we are still refining oil that was (4. sold) ______________ while prices were high – and petrol prices were too low." Blackbourn went on to describe the fluctuations in the price of crude oil and to explain how that impacted the market and the oil companies. "We are vulnerable to the vagaries of the market, too," he concluded.

"How (5. slowly) ________________ should prices go back down for (6. producers) ________________."

"Do I look like Nostradamus?" he asked almost angrily. "I can't predict that," he (7. stopped) ________________ more peacefully, "but I would think that within the next few weeks, there should be a bit of a (8. rise) ________________ in prices."

"A slight (9. increase) ______________ in prices, then, within a month?"

"Possibly. I don't have a crystal ball, Mr Rogers."
"Moving on to another subject," Flowers said, crossing his legs, "what do you know about Beyond 2050?"
"They're an environmental organisation. They're not quite as active as Greenpeace and some of the other ones, but they're – what should I say? – they're active too."
"What is your relationship with them?"
"What is our relationship with Beyond 2050? We have no relationship with them. They and other environmental organisations challenge us to meet higher standards and we try to meet those standards. But we have no special relationship with Beyond 2050 – or any of the other groups."
Despite this "umbrella" answer, Flowers asked about other environmental and consumer organisations and got similar answers.
"I'm really out of time, Mr Rogers. I said ten minutes and that's all I could spare. I really have to ask you to leave."
"One last question, if you please. How closely do you work with First Sea Oil?"
"How *closely* do we work with them?" Blackbourn looked completely surprised by the question.
"Exactly," Flowers responded, ignoring Blackbourn's apparent surprise.
"We don't work *with* them, Mr Rogers, we compete *against* them. They happen to be our number one competitor."
"So there have been no meetings with them?"
"Not at all. Where did you hear that we had?"
"Rumours, that's all, among the environmental organisations."

"Naturally. Well, you can put that rumour to rest. There have been no meetings between First Oil and Golden Day."

"Okay, Mr Blackbourn, thank you for your time," Flowers said and switched the cassette player off.

"I'll look forward to reading your article in the *Guardian* or is it the *Independent*?"

"*The Guardian*. I can find my way out," Flowers said after shaking Blackbourn's hand.

ÜBUNG 34 !

Übung 34: Fügen Sie das richtige Substantiv in die Sätze ein! ***(relationship, challenge, rumour, crystal ball, subject, standard, competitor)***

1. A glass globe to see the future is a ________________.
2. A topic to be discussed is a ________________.
3. An association between people is a ________________.
4. A demanding or difficult task is a ________________.
5. A measure by which the quality of others is judged is a ________________.
6. A person who is a rival in business is a ________________.
7. Public talk of doubtful accuracy is a ________________.

Blackbourn nodded, and Flowers walked out of his office, past his secretary and into the hallway. He stood a moment looking both ways down the hallway. 'Where should I go next?' he wondered. Suddenly, a door opened and out came two security guards wearing

midnight blue uniforms with golden badges on the shoulder and dark blue hats.
"Hello Mr Rogers," said one. "We're here to escort you out of the building."
"That's not necessary. I can – "

Übung 35: Ordnen Sie die Buchstaben zu einem sinnvollen Wort!

"Please come with us," the same person said, his hand firmly taking hold of Flowers' elbow, and leading Flowers to the (1. tilf) __________. The doors opened and he said, "After you," and (2. turedges) _______________ for Flowers to enter, which he did.

"So what's it like working for Britain's second largest oil (3. pacomny) _______________?"

"It's a job," the first (4. ardug) __________ answered.

"Your (5. eagollcue) ____________ doesn't speak?"

"Not if he doesn't have to, isn't that right Paul?" Paul just looked back, expressionless. "See what I mean?"

"Maybe he's just saving his (6. rengey) __________," Flowers said, turning to the doors and looking away from the two security guards.

"Maybe I am saving it," Paul said at last in a sandpaper voice that was clearly threatening. "There are sometimes people who are not what they say they are and we have to be (7. lfureac) ________________ with them."

"I can understand that," Flowers said and added, "you can't be too careful."

Chapter 4: Digging Deeper

"We've had quite a busy day," Blood said to Flowers as Flowers walked in the front door in the early afternoon. "Earlier John Glaser was on duty once again."
"My old friend Inspector Glaser," Flowers said. "Did he have any success?"
"I don't know. And Mr Rogers, reporter for the *Independent*, did he have any success?"
"First of all, he's a reporter for the *Guardian*," Flowers said. "I don't know. I feel like I got nothing and only alerted him to something, that someone has suspicions about the Big 3."
"Maybe it will force them to act."
"More likely it'll force them to go even deeper underground. How was your visit to the First Sea refinery?"

ÜBUNG 36 !

Übung 36: Unterstreichen Sie das „schwarze Schaf"!

1. to escort, to accompany, to lead, to follow
2. office, hallway, corridor, passage
3. duty, work, transfer, obligation
4. to play, to act, to perform, to operate
5. demand, demonstration, request, need

"Wisacker, the assistant director of the refinery, was oddly hostile. I don't know if he was simply in a bad mood, but he was at times confrontational and at other times helpful. Sometimes I was suspicious of him and thought perhaps he feared me, which might explain his hostility. Other times I thought he realized I was there to help him – or at least as far as he knew I was – but that only lasted a few minutes. You know, I didn't realize that the banner was hung at night – I know it's only common sense, but somehow that escaped me. Naturally, most organisations do these things in daylight so they can get as much attention as possible. There were no signs of illegal entry and the fence is so high that climbing it would be quite difficult."

Übung 37: Verbessern Sie die falsch geschriebenen Wörter!

"If it were somebody inside the company," Flowers said, "then the problem is (1. soulved) __________ . They got in the normal way, drove through in a company car and put the banner up and left."

"Perhaps we should speak with the security (2. gards) __________ on duty that night. I have their names. Sally," Blood said, "could you get (3. adresses) ____________ for these four names?"

"Anything else?" Flowers asked.

"I wonder what else is in the (4. storege arier) ______________.

There were boxes right behind the Beyond 2050 banner that were big enough to (5. contayn) __________ other banners. How are banners (6. deliverd) __________? Are they folded into squares and rolled up?"

"You've got me," Flowers responded.

"Isn't it a little late to be coming to the plant, Inspector?" the guard asked after looking at Inspector Glaser's identification.
"I have to do my work when I have the time. Besides, since when is 7pm late? You're still up, right mate? How late do you work?"
"Me? I work until midnight."
Blood was sitting in his car and held his list up to the guard. "Is anyone on the list on duty?"
"Robert Parks is on duty tonight – and Simon Greenblatt is too."
"Well, then, I would like to be allowed in so that I can speak with them."
"I have to ask."
"Go on, ask whoever you like."
A minute later, Blood was walking from the car park to the Security Office. It was just getting dark and the temperature was sinking quickly. In the background, the refinery was reddish-orange. Blood opened the door and walked in.
"Inspector Glaser?" a tall man with red curly hair asked.
Blood nodded 'yes' and the man held out the telephone receiver.
"Inspector Glaser," Blood said into the telephone.
"Robert Wisacker here."
"Hello Mr Wisacker, what can I do for you?"
"I was calling to ask what I could do for you."
"Nothing, sir. I'm not here to speak to you. I'm here to speak to some members of your security team."
"I thought I asked you to speak to them when they're off duty."
"You did, Mr Wisacker, but I'm going to speak to two of them presently."

Übung 38: Übersetzen Sie!

1. Wie lange arbeiten Sie gewöhnlich?

2. Er hielt ihm den Telefonhörer hin.

3. Wer hat heute abend Dienst?

4. Er hat von seinem Arbeitgeber einen Firmenwagen bekommen.

5. Die Waren sind in der Lagerhalle.

Blood heard a loud sigh of frustration. "I'd like to speak to them first, if you don't mind."

"Okay, I'll put you on speaker phone," Blood said and without waiting for objections he pressed a button and suddenly Wisacker was able to address the three security guards and Blood all at the same time. "Go on," Blood said, "they're listening."

"I didn't ask you to put me on the speaker phone, Inspector."

"That's okay, Mr Wisacker," Blood answered, ignoring the implicit complaint.

"Parks and Greenblatt," Wisacker's voice took on an even more stringent tone, "don't neglect your duties while speaking to the Inspector."

"No sir, we won't," they said, one after the other.

"You don't need to be told that one more blunder like the other night and your careers with First Sea are over."
The two men rolled their eyes but said, "yes, sir."
Wisacker hung up without saying goodbye.

ÜBUNG 39 !

Übung 39: Setzen Sie die richtige Präposition ein!
(on 2x, to 2x, up, at 2x)

1. Blood talked about his visit _______ the First Sea refinery.
2. Who was _______ duty yesterday?
3. I would like to speak _______ Mr. Greenblatt.
4. Angrily, he hung _______ the phone.
5. Their careers _______ First Sea were nearly over.
6. Would you please put him _______ the speaker phone?
7. The guard was looking ______ Glaser's identification.

"He's not our boss," the red-haired man said. "He might be one day, but he ain't now. I'm Greenblatt, Simon Greenblatt."
"And I'm Robert Parks," said a younger man with a small moustache and long sideburns of the style that were popular in the 1970s.
"And I'm Inspector Glaser, as you probably know already. I wanted to ask you about the other night again, the night when the banner was hung."
"That was rather embarrassing," Greenblatt said. "But we couldn't do anything about it. We watched the monitors as closely as you can, but you can't stare at them for hours without looking away

occasionally. We just must have had bad luck."
"That's right," said Parks. "If those environmental groups want to do something, they can usually find a way to do it. It's a game of cat and mouse for them."
"But we're the mice," Greenblatt said, "me and Parks and the other guards."
"But it *is* hard to believe that you didn't see them climbing the chimney with the banner."

Übung 40: Unterstreichen Sie die richtige Alternative!

ÜBUNG 40 !

"It just (1.) depends on/relies on which cameras you've got on the (2.) TV/screen at a given moment. We have other areas that we monitor more closely. I can't tell you which, but there are areas that the (3.) management/CEO have told us to focus on."
"Was there any unusual activity that night – did any cars come in late or were there any late (4.) shops/deliveries?"
"Deliveries can come any time, day or night, that's usual."
"Did any cars come in?"
"No, but a few (5.) lorries/ambulances did. Nothing strange though."
"And the next morning there were no signs of forced (6.) entry/admission?"

"None that I know of," Greenblatt answered and looked questioningly at Parks who shook his head 'no' as well.
"How do you think they got the sign to the top?"
"That's a good question," Parks responded. "There are padlocks on the ladders, and you can't get up there without the ladders."
"Actually," said Greenblatt, "there are only two places where you

need keys to get to where they hung the sign."
"And the locks are still in place?"
"As far as I know they are."
"How many sets of keys are there?"
"A lot. Just about everybody who works in the plant has a key."
"Any keys reported missing?"
"No, sir."
"Can I see yours?" Blood asked.
Greenblatt pulled out a big ring of keys and selected one. "Here it is."
Blood studied it for a moment. There was nothing unusual about the key except, perhaps, that "Do not duplicate" was not engraved on it. "And yours?" Parks pulled out a key that looked identical. "Mr Parks," Blood said, addressing the young man of about 25, "could you escort me to the area where the banner is being stored?"
"I'm not sure where that is," he said.
"I'll lead you. You just bring your keys."

ÜBUNG 41 !

Übung 41: Bringen Sie die Wörter in die richtige Reihenfolge!

1. management guards certain told the the security on to focus areas

____

2. late were other night the deliveries there

____

3. working set everybody the keys plant had at a of

____

4. missing were keys no reported

___

5. guard Blood the storage asked young the him area to to escort

___

Parks looked at Greenblatt, as if for support, but Greenblatt looked back stonily.
"But, but," Parks began, not moving a step.
"But what?" Blood said, raising himself to his full height. "Is there a problem?"
"We didn't get clear orders to let you back there," Greenblatt finally explained.
"That's right. But you didn't get clear orders *not* to let me back there, is that right?"
The two men shrugged their shoulders, so Blood began walking and Parks fell in behind him. In the hallway, Blood asked, "so, Mr Parks, how long have you worked here?"
"I've been here four years now."
"And before that?"
"I worked the door at a nightclub. One night I had a difficulty with a coked-up rock star and that was the end."

Übung 42: Finden Sie Synonyme zu den Wörtern in Klammern!

"So you've (1. been employed) ___________ here for four years as security guard? You've had the same (2. position) ___________ the whole time?"

"Yes, for the most part. I've been in Security the whole time. I also used to work at the front (3. gate) _______________ sometimes, (4. checking) _____________ the (5. lorries) __________ as they came in, but I don't do that anymore."

"Any (6. chance) _____________ of someone catching a ride with a lorry into the refinery?"

"I reckon anything is possible. You would just have to keep your head low and your mouth shut while the guard is going through the (7. papers) ____________."

"How many people could get in?"
"Two at most, I should think. Most of the lorries don't have sleeping compartments in them. They don't drive that far."
"But some do have these sleeping compartments?"
"Yes, some do. Maybe a quarter of them."
They stopped at the door and Blood waited while Parks opened the door. He pushed the door open and held it for Blood to enter first. The lights went on and Blood saw that the banner was now gone though everything else was in place. Instead of mentioning the missing banner, however, he walked immediately over to the boxes and opened one.
"I don't know that you should really do that, sir," Parks said.
"Just checking things out, Parks," he answered and then added: "You can turn your head if it makes you nervous, mate."
Inside the box were chemicals. He lifted a bottle. On the label was a sun coming up just over the horizon in a blaze of gold. Pulling it up a bit farther, he saw that it was some sort of additive.
"What's this?"
"No idea, sir. I just work in Security."

"What's in the plastic barrels?"
"Like I said …."
Blood put his hands on the barrels and noticed that they were empty.
"So, could you tell me where the banner is?" Blood asked at last. "It was in here a few hours ago."
They looked in several cabinets but came up empty. One, however, was locked and after trying several keys it became clear that Parks did not have the key.

Übung 43: Übersetzen Sie und enträtseln Sie das Lösungswort!

1. Abteil _ _ _ _ □ _ _ _ _ _ _
2. Anweisung _ _ □ _ _
3. anstatt _ _ _ _ _ _ □
4. Posten _ _ _ □ _ _ _ _
5. betreten _ _ □ _ _
6. vervielfältigen _ _ _ _ □ _ _ _ _
7. Lieferung _ _ _ _ □ _ _ _
8. Raffinerie _ _ _ _ _ □ _ _

Lösung: _ _ _ _ _ _ _ _

"Hmm," the young man said. "I'm supposed to have a key for everything."
"The bosses have to have their secrets, eh Parks? Are there any other rooms where it could be stored?"
"I reckon there are a few others we could try," he answered. They went to those, too, and came up with nothing, no banner and nothing that looked interesting to Blood.

"This is everything, young Mr Parks?" Parks nodded his head 'yes'. "I'll be very unhappy with you if I find out differently," Blood added.
"It's the truth, Inspector. I don't know any other place where it could be."
"Let's go back," Blood said at last. They returned to the office.
"Did Wisacker phone back?" Blood asked. Greenblatt's face gave him away immediately. "What did he ask? Come on, lad," Blood said, though Greenblatt could not be more than a few years younger than him.
"He just asked where you were and what we had told you, Inspector Glaser."
"Why do you think he asked that?"
Both men looked at him and shrugged their shoulders.

ÜBUNG 44 !

Übung 44: Verbinden Sie die Verben mit den Substantiven zu sinnvollen Ausdrücken!

1. to have	☐ her/his shoulders
2. to nod	☐ a colleague
3. to shrug	☐ a secret
4. to get	☐ the plant
5. to work	☐ orders
6. to address	☐ long hours
7. to employ	☐ his head
8. to monitor	☐ a security guard

"Is there something he doesn't want you to tell me? If there is and I get it through another source I'm going to make life difficult for you and Wisacker. I'll make it difficult for First Sea in general."

"I've no idea what he would *not* want us to say," Greenblatt replied. After a bit more discussion, Blood left without obtaining any further information. Outside it was dark, and the refinery was lit with green and violet lights. It's quite beautiful at night, he thought. That's modern art right there – industrial and functional.

Chapter 5: Hot Talk

"Did you see the news last night?" Fielding asked Flowers.
"No. Did I miss something?"
"Well, I don't know for sure, but I think so. Did you hear that there were protests about petrol prices in London yesterday? Future Watch and other groups, among them Beyond 2050, are finally beginning to become more active on the issue."
"There was brief mention of that on the radio this morning."
"There was an interview with one of the leaders, a woman from I don't know which group, who called for governmental oversight. They want the government to investigate why prices have gone up and are continuing to go up. And you have to admit," Fielding added, "prices always go up at Christmas and Easter and right at the beginning of school holidays in July, as if perfectly planned and coordinated. They're right, you know. It's really suspicious. Good luck finding cheap petrol at Easter."

Übung 45: Bilden Sie aus den Adjektiven Substantive!

1. industrial ________________

2. functional ________________

ÜBUNG 45 !

3. leading ____________________

4. governmental ____________________

5. investigative ____________________

6. perfect ____________________

Half an hour later, Blood came in, carrying a small television.
"You're late, Dave," Fielding said, "and you're carrying a telly."
"I was working late last night, Sally," he explained.
"Did you find out anything new?" Flowers called out from his office.

ÜBUNG 46

Übung 46: Unterstreichen Sie die richtige Alternative!

"Let's just say they've aroused some new (1.) suspicions/investigations. The banner was gone and they're using (2.) deliveries/products from Golden Day Oil."
Flowers walked out to Sally Fielding's (3.) desk/table. "What's with the telly? I heard you say something about (4.) working/getting up late, but you're not going to catch up on telly here, are you?"
"Funny, Flowers. If you had a telly you'd know that at 10am this morning there's going to be (5.) a press conference/an interview where the environmental groups are going to officially call on the government to investigate the price increases. Future Watch is (6.) following/leading the whole thing, but I want to see who else is (7.) involved/employed."

"I was telling Kevin about that," Fielding said.
"You're our eyes and ears, Sally," Flowers said.
"Sometimes I am," she answered. "Someone has to be when the

two of you are running about like headless chickens. And you," she continued, addressing Flowers, "without a telly, you rely on Blood and me to keep you up on things."
Blood smiled at Flowers and then hooked up the television and turned it on.
"Should be on in a little bit."

Übung 47: Welche ist die richtige Bedeutung der englischen Redewendungen? Kreuzen Sie an!

1. You are our eyes and ears.
   a) ☐ You are too curious.
   b) ☐ You watch and listen carefully to find out what's going on.

2. They are running about like headless chickens.
   a) ☐ They are running about directionless.
   b) ☐ They are dancing wildly because they are very happy.

3. We are trying all avenues.
   a) ☐ We're doing whatever it takes to achieve the best result possible.
   b) ☐ We're wasting a lot of time to reach the best result possible.

4. Should be on in a little bit.
   a) ☐ We should go soon.
   b) ☐ It should start in a few minutes.

5. Good luck finding cheap petrol.
   a) ☐ You can't find cheap petrol.
   b) ☐ The petrol prices are really low.

"It's beginning," Fielding called to them, and Flowers and Blood rushed out to Fielding's desk.

"You see anyone familiar?" Fielding asked, her voice rising, which signified that she did see someone familiar.

There on the panel alongside leaders of Future Watch and several other groups sat Preston Stiles, tall and isolated. He was off to one side, but during the course of the press conference he made his presence known. Invited at last to speak, he looked at the cameras with a serious expression, put his notes down, lifted his glasses onto his forehead and began.

"I wonder," he said, "if there's something illegal going on between the oil companies, especially the three largest producers. I wonder if they're working together to raise prices not only for their petrol stations but for all petrol stations across England and, indeed, the UK. I think this is something that the government should be looking into – "

"He's got us looking into that," Blood said.

"No, that's not our job," Flowers whispered, "and we need to remember that. We're only trying to find out who – "

"Hush, you two," Fielding said quickly, "and listen."

ÜBUNG 48 !

Übung 48: Sind die folgenden Aussagen richtig ✔ oder falsch – ?

1. Finally, there were protests in London about the high petrol prices. ☐
2. The environmental groups were no longer passively watching the price increases. ☐
3. The government was starting an official investigation. ☐
4. Blood wanted to watch a TV documentary in his office. ☐
5. Future Watch led the protests for the environmental groups. ☐

6. Preston Stiles was the main speaker at the press conference. ☐
7. The oil companies want the government to investigate the raise in oil prices. ☐
8. The oil prices always go up after the summer holidays in July. ☐

"The Prime Minister is too focused on international affairs that don't really concern us at the moment. He's got to come back here and see what's going on in merry old England, see what's going on in his own backyard. It's clear to all that he's focusing on Africa and Asia and wherever, so we now have oil companies who think they can do whatever they bloody well like with impunity. We're here today to put a stop to all that, right here, right now. Mr Prime Minister, it's time to get to work for the people who put you in office – not tomorrow or next month but today, this morning, this minute. We put you in office and we can send you right back to the family farm you were born on."
"He's good," Fielding said, as the moderator now asked another leader to speak.
"Regulatory oversight," she began, "has been a disaster. No one is monitoring the monitors. What, if anything, are they doing? What are their interests, because they don't seem to be looking out for ours? The people who are supposed to be serving us are failing in their duties."

Blood, Flowers and Fielding watched the entire press conference.
"He's good-looking," Fielding said, referring to Stiles, "when he gets passionate."
"If he'd just take those dumb glasses off his forehead," Blood suggested, "he might look even better."
"You're both so superficial," Flowers began.

ÜBUNG 49 !

Übung 49: Unterstreichen Sie das „schwarze Schaf“!

1. to focus, to forward, to target, to concentrate
2. to confirm, to concern, to be about, to be connected with
3. to indicate, to signify, to express, to explain
4. producer, creator, consumer, fabricator
5. supervisor, monitor, guard, guarantee
6. to serve, to help, to assist, to miss

"Well, he does have something. I knew that when I first saw him; I just wasn't sure what it was."

"I can hardly believe it," Blood said, "you going on like that."

"I suppose being around the two of you would be enough to do the damage."

"Now, we have to focus on what Stiles hired us for," Flowers said.

"But the two things are not separate," Blood answered. "These companies are working together and they want the environmental groups to look bad. It goes together."

"You see that, and I see that. I'm sure he sees that, too. But he wants us to focus on their attack on the group. I reckon he thinks he can handle the other issue – and besides, remember? he wanted us to inform Scotland Yard, Mac, so that they would know the latest developments. They can do the work they're paid to do and we'll do the work he's paying us to do."

"Well, it should be quite easy," Blood said, disappointed, "to do what he wants us to do."

"It should," Flowers agreed, "and yet we can't find any connection. What is it we're looking for?"

"They're not exactly going to have signs up saying, we did it."

"I think we should visit Beyond 2050's offices and see what they think."

Übung 50: Übersetzen Sie!

1. Dafür wurden wir nicht engagiert!

2. Wir sollten uns auf unsere Arbeit konzentrieren!

3. Ich glaube, wir können die Angelegenheit regeln!

4. Wir möchten über die neuesten Entwicklungen informiert werden!

5. Niemand kontrolliert die Überwacher!

The offices for Beyond 2050 were located far away from Oxford Street and Piccadilly Circus, on the outskirts of a part of London where many small businesses were located. The two detectives walked calmly along the street.
"Looks quite nice," Blood said, standing in front of the building. "They've done quite well. I wonder which floor they're on," Blood wondered.
"That's a good question," Flowers said. He pushed a button to be allowed in.
"Yes," said a voice.
"This is Blood and Flowers, we were hired by Mr Stiles."
"Oh, yes, right, come right in."

ÜBUNG 51 !

Übung 51: Ordnen Sie die Buchstaben zu einem sinnvollen Wort!

The door (1. uzzbed) ________________ and the two men walked in. Straight ahead was a (2. filt) ___________. They waited for it and inside they noticed that while several companies had offices on each floor, only two shared the third floor, Beyond 2050 and the (3. rabchn) ___________ office of an (4. rancuinse) _____________ company.

"They're doing pretty well," Flowers remarked, "if they can (5. droffa) ___________ a large office."

"Who knows? It might be quite small."

They got off at the third floor and walked to some (6. sslag roods) ____________________ with Beyond 2050 written across them. A young man standing behind the doors opened them as soon as he saw Flowers and Blood.

"Good afternoon, my name is Justin Rhyes-Davies."
"I'm Kevin Flowers."
"And I'm David Blood. Are you Mr Stiles' assistant?"
"Yes, you could say I am."
"What would you say you are?" Blood asked.
"I reckon I'd say I was Mr Stiles' assistant as well."
"Good. Mr Stiles hired us to find out about the banner at First Sea Oil, among other things," Flowers said. "You have quite a nice office," he added. "You must have a lot of donor members."

"We do," he said, "but I have nothing to do with how much this costs and all that. Stiles handles all that himself."

"I'd expect you to have an accountant."

"So, how many people work here?"

"There are five of us."

"And what do you do?"

"We keep up on current events and update our website daily with our activities and with activities of interest to our members. We also have people who come here for meetings, planning future activities."

"And those people are mainly volunteers?" Blood asked.

"No, we pay our organisers. How can we expect them to focus on our interests and those of our members if they spend all their time working just to live? They've got to have energy. If nothing else, the pay gives them the energy to work full-time and then work with us, too."

"That's quite noble of you."

Übung 52: Vervollständigen Sie die Sätze!

ÜBUNG 52 !

1. If somebody works the entire legal work-time he works ________________.

2. Somebody who gives money to an organisation so that it can fulfil certain goals is a ________________.

3. A professional responsible for the records of money received or spent by a company is an ________________.

4. A person who offers his services to an organisation without having the duty to do this is a ________________.

5. Somebody who makes arrangements or brings affairs into order is an ______________.

6. Somebody who helps someone else to do a job is an ________.

7. A person whose job it is to investigate and discover information about people is a ______________.

Rhyes-Davies nodded in acknowledgement of the compliment.
"We heard that you had a computer virus recently that seems to have come from a hostile source."
"Well, it's not clear where it came from," Rhyes-Davies admitted. "It really wasn't so bad. With the help of our programmers, I was able to have it removed within two days. It ate a lot of files, but it wasn't as bad as some I've heard of. I suppose we're on the internet so often that it's always possible. We've now upgraded our firewall and our antivirus programmes, so that sort of thing shouldn't happen again."
"And your assets were frozen?" Blood asked.
The young man shrugged his shoulders. "I've nothing to do with finances and I never heard any mention of our finances being frozen. I've got my salary each month and as far as I know so has everyone else."
"You never heard anything about this?" Flowers asked, frowning. "That's odd. You are second in charge here?"
"Yes, but, really, Mr Stiles handles everything himself. He tells me what to do and I do it. Nothing more and nothing less. He's a good boss. We discuss activities, he provides me with objectives and we review the action plan. Sometimes he's a bit impulsive, but generally he's motivating and adventurous. Some find him charismatic, and if you look at his achievement – building Beyond 2050 in less than three years – he really is something else."

Übung 53: Welche Wörter haben eine ähnliche Bedeutung? Setzen Sie die entsprechende Ziffer ein!

ÜBUNG 53 !

1. assets	☐ accomplishment
2. finances	☐ earnings
3. salary	☐ scheme
4. charge	☐ aim
5. objective	☐ duty
6. achievement	☐ capital
7. plan	☐ money
8. investigation	☐ origin
9. source	☐ study

"So, where is everyone?" Blood asked.
"They went to the press conference this morning and I don't know where they are now."
"Why did you have to stay here? Why didn't you go along?"
"Someone had to be here to answer phones and questions and to be here to greet visitors," Rhyes-Davies answered.
"Good point."

Chapter 6: Rogers Swings Back into Action

"More news," Fielding said, as Blood and Flowers returned to the office. "Future Watch is about to be investigated by the Controller's Office."
"Was any reason given?"
"The news was only that the decision had been made several days earlier so the investigation had nothing to do with the press conference."

ÜBUNG 54 !

Übung 54: Setzen Sie die Ausdrücke in Klammern in die Lücken ein!

(appointment, unfamiliar, information, passed, in, leave, around, give)

"I wonder," said Flowers, "if it had anything to do with the information I (1.) __________ on to Mac."

"(2.) __________ him a call," Blood suggested.

"I'd like to speak to James Ireland," Flowers said, when an (3.) ____________ voice answered. "Is Mac (4.) __________?"

"He's not at his desk at the moment."

"Do you expect him (5.) ________ later?"

"I don't know. I haven't seen him today."

"Okay. Could you just (6.) __________ a message that Kevin Flowers called. Ask him to call me back, if you would."

"Will do."

"Goodbye. Dave," Flowers said, walking out of his office. "If Mac calls back, ask him if he knows anything about the investigation into Future Watch – and ask if it has anything to do with the (7.) __________ we gave him."

"No problem," Blood answered. "Are you going somewhere?"

"Yes, I'm going to P-Ride to speak with Julian Rath."

"You got an (8.) _______________?"

"I'm going to get one."
The P-Ride – which was pronounced "pride" by consumers and employees alike – headquarters were in central London, so Flowers took the underground to their offices.
"I'm Jimmy Rogers from *The Guardian*," he said to the receptionist, showing her his identification, "and I would like to speak with Mr Julian Rath."
"Do you have an appointment?"
"No, I don't. If you tell him I'm with *The Guardian* I'm sure he'll be willing to speak with me."
The receptionist picked up the phone and dialled a number. "There's a reporter here to speak with Mr Rath. Yes, he's from the *Guardian*. Yes, I've seen his identification and it looks like it's all in order. Yes, I'll ask. Your name, sir?" she asked, addressing Flowers. "Jimmy Rogers."
"Did you get that? Okay, I'll send him up." She put the phone down and said, "He's on the 8th floor, room 821. The lift is just there," she said, pointing. "Here's a visitor's pass. Please make sure it's visible at all times."
"Thank you," Flowers said and walked over to the lift. He got off at the eighth floor and walked around until he found Rath's office.

Übung 55: Welche Synonyme gehören zusammen? Ordnen Sie zu!

1. appointment	☐ credentials
2. lift	☐ receptionist
3. identification	☐ staff
4. pass	☐ engagement
5. employees	☐ elevator
6. desk clerk	☐ permit

There were many offices and they all appeared to be filled. People walking past him ignored him. "Hello," he said, entering room 821. "I'm Jimmy Rogers from the *Guardian*."
"Please take a seat, Mr Rogers," said a dark-haired woman of about 35, wearing a dark blue business suit with trousers. "Mr Rath is on the phone at the moment."
"You're his secretary?"
"I'm his personal assistant," she corrected.
"So you attend meetings with him?"
"Frequently but not always."
"Were you at the meeting recently between P-Ride, First Sea Oil and Golden Day?"
"How did? – what? – Mr Rogers, you had better save your questions for Mr Rath."
"Did you discuss the environmental groups like Future Watch or Beyond 2050?"
"We don't talk about them at all unless they're leading a protest."
"So, you don't deny that such a meeting took place?"
"Look, I'm not authorised to speak to reporters for the company, but Mr Rath is, so perhaps you'd be so kind as to…" she stopped speaking and turned her back to him.
Flowers decided not to press her any further. He already had more than he had expected to get.

ÜBUNG 56 !

Übung 56: Setzen Sie die richtigen Präpositionen ein!
(in 3x, on 2x, into, from)

"Mr Rath is off the phone now." She stood, knocked gently (1.) _____ the door, then Flowers was led (2.) _____ a relatively small office. Standing up behind the desk was a man with bleached blond hair and a moustache that matched it perfectly. He was (3.) _____ his late 50s or early 60s, but still seemed a bit young. Flowers thought he would look equally at home (4.) _____ a swimsuit (5.) _____ a surfboard, despite his age and somewhat stocky build.

"Sorry to keep you waiting," he said (6.) _____ a friendly manner, "Mr –?"

"Rogers, Jimmy Rogers, (7.) _____ the *Guardian*," he said, extending his hand.

"Rath," he said, taking hold of Flowers' hand. "What can I do for you, Mr Rogers?" Mr Rath asked.

"Do you mind?" Flowers asked, pulling out the cassette player and lifting it up for Rath to see.

"Go ahead," Rath answered, "although whenever people listen to those things they always find I've made different statements from those I remember making. Curious, isn't it?" he said with an ironic smile.

"It is," Flowers said with a smile, but after more than a decade as a bobby he was not a person to be won by youth and friendliness, not even in a man old enough to be his father. "I'd like to speak to you today about your relationship with some of the environmental groups and a few related topics."

"Yes, I saw the press conference this morning."

"What did you think of their request that the government look into the current oil and petrol prices?"

He shrugged his shoulders. "It's nothing new and if the government wants to investigate the prices, then it should. We at P-Ride have no objections and nothing to hide."

"How do you explain the high prices?"

"Why do I have to, Mr Rogers?" he asked playfully. They looked at each other silently – Rath smiling. "Have you ever gone into an off-license and asked the cashier to explain their prices? Have you ever questioned a restaurant manager about the prices in a restaurant? We can charge what the market will bear – isn't that what free enterprise is all about? If people don't like our prices they are perfectly free to go somewhere else. Naturally," he added quickly, "we hope they won't go somewhere else – but they can."

"And there is always the tube and the train."

"Exactly," he agreed, carelessly. "Consumers come in all shapes and sizes."

"But isn't there a difference between the market share of a restaurant or an off-license and the market share of an oil company?"

"That's just the nature of this particular market. These are the conditions and we have to live and function within them."

ÜBUNG 57 !

Übung 57: Welche Definition enthält die richtige Bedeutung? Kreuzen Sie an!

1. market segment
   a) ☐ a group of consumers
   b) ☐ a group of products
   c) ☐ a group of men

2. market share
   a) ☐ percentage of automobiles in use
   b) ☐ amount of money in circulation

c) ☐ comparison based on competitors in a particular market

3. market gap
   a) ☐ insufficient supply of a product
   b) ☐ a product not on offer but desired
   c) ☐ distance between product development and market

4. consumer profile
   a) ☐ typical customer
   b) ☐ consumer information
   c) ☐ customer appearance

5. turnover
   a) ☐ profit
   b) ☐ loss
   c) ☐ money that comes in and out of a company

"So, these protests don't worry you?" Flowers asked.

"Why should they? Our prices may be higher than they were a few weeks ago, but they're still fair and people are still buying. I don't have the latest sales figures, but I don't believe our sales have been hurt in any way by the high prices. The environmental groups just want to start a little controversy, so what's the harm?"

"How closely do you work with First Sea Oil and Golden Day or any of the other oil companies?"

"We are competitors and nothing more," Rath answered, dismissively.

"You don't work with them?"

"Naturally we watch each other to see what new products the other is launching on the market."

"It seems that your prices always go up together."

"Everybody's prices go up at about the same time."
"So, you deny that there's any, shall we say, coordination going on?"
"That would be illegal."
"And yet I've got information that a meeting did indeed take place in which senior executives of P-Ride met with Golden Day and First Sea. What do you say to that?"
"I would be interested to know where you got that information and to know who attended the meeting."

Übung 58: Setzen Sie die Verben in die richtige Zeitform!

Flowers stared at Rath, (1. stun) __________ for a moment. He's as cool as a cucumber, he (2. think) __________. "Perhaps," Flowers said at last, "*you* could tell me."

"I know of no such meeting," Rath answered with a smile, "so I (3. not/can) __________ give you any more information."

"It (4. will) __________ perhaps surprise you to know, then, that you are on the list of people who attended."

"That does surprise me," he said with a smile. "But it doesn't bother me."

(5. say/you) " _____________ that the meeting never took place?"

"Yes."

"Even though two people who (6. be) __________ at the meeting say you were there, too."

"I can't change what other people say, Mr – ?"

"Rogers," Flowers said. (7. have/you) "_______________ contact with any of the environmental groups?"

"Only when they hang signs from our refineries – but that hasn't happened in a while. Actually," Rath continued, "if you want some real news, a 'scoop' as you call it in the newspaper trade, I believe I have something that might be of interest to you: two people tried to get in here last night and hang a banner from the top of our building. They managed to enter the building and get to the stairs and were about halfway up when they were stopped."
"Your security seems a bit lax."
"Perhaps. Or these people were good at what they do."
"Were you able to identify them and which group they work for?" Flowers asked.
"No, I'm afraid they managed to escape. One of the guards almost got a backpack off one of them but he was beaten down. His injuries were minor, so he was treated at the hospital and released."
"And you reported this to the police?"
"Of course. They spoke to a few people immediately after the break-in attempt, but I wasn't one of them. I wasn't around at that hour of the night, though it sometimes feels as if I am always here. But even after 28 years of marriage my wife still wants me at home in the evening, if you can imagine that."

Übung 59: Ordnen Sie die Buchstaben zu einem sinnvollen Wort!

1. Another word for workforce is (ftasf) __________.

2. Bosses are sometimes also called (sangrema) _______________.

3. A profession can sometimes be called a (drate) __________.

4. If I don't have permission to do something I am not (thaursoide) __________.

5. The opposite of minor is (roajm) __________.

6. People who ensure the safety of a building and the employees are (cesturiy) __________.

"So," Flowers said, changing the subject, "do you find any of the environmental groups particularly annoying, say, for example, Future Watch or Beyond 2050?"

The man looked at Flowers closely, for the first time dropping the appearance of light-heartedness. "I think I've already answered that question. You just asked the question differently."

"But don't you agree that the oil companies would like to discredit some of these groups?"

"These environmental groups usually discredit themselves; they don't need our help."

"So you deny working with or, better said, against any particular environmental group or set of groups?"

"You know, Mr Rogers, you sound more like a policeman than a reporter."

"Reporters perform a service similar to that of the police. Ever since Woodward and Bernstein exposed the corruption of the Nixon administration in 1972–1974, generally known as Watergate, investigative reporters have seen it as their duty to expose illegal activities. I'm simply following in that tradition."

"Well, I have no illegal activities to report, except the one which we were almost a victim of last night."

"Do you know about any illegal activities on the part of your competitors?"
"Mr Rogers, you are the investigative reporter. You have to dig up that information."
Seeing that there was nothing more to be gained at the moment, Flowers decided to end the interview. He switched the cassette player off.
"Thank you for your time, Mr Rath," he said, once again offering his hand. "The pleasure was all mine," Mr Rath answered, shaking Flowers' hand.

Übung 60: Finden Sie das Gegenteil und setzen Sie die richtige Ziffer ein!

ÜBUNG 60

1. lax	☐ confusion
2. discredit	☐ discriminatory
3. personal	☐ strict
4. coordination	☐ indifference
5. concern	☐ distant
6. fair	☐ respect

Flowers left Rath's office and this time went straight to the lift. As he left the building, a group of people were also coming out. People in blue suits and black suits came out behind him, some went in one direction, some in another, and some stood around. Flowers paused in front of the building looking up at the sky and then in several directions, figuring out exactly where he was.
"Excuse me, Mr Rogers," called a female voice.
Flowers didn't turn around until he felt an arm on his shoulder. "Oh, hello," he said to Rath's personal assistant.

"Hello. You are not going to report that I confirmed a meeting between the three biggest oil companies are you?" She did not ask this question as if she were worried; she was not asking this question from a position of weakness. There could be no doubt that she would not beg Flowers/Rogers not to print the information: she would only dispute it.
"A meeting between the Big 3? I would like to be able to prove it, but I can't – not just yet."
"Good," she said and turning around walked back into the building. As the sun was shining, he decided to walk back to the office which was about three kilometres away. He began walking.

! ÜBUNG 61

Übung 61: Welches Wort ist das „schwarze Schaf"? Unterstreichen Sie das nicht in die Reihe passende Wort!

1. disagreement, conflict, quarrel, confront
2. confirm, refute, substantiate, verify
3. tell, reproduce, report, inform
4. limitation, disadvantage, limitless, weakness
5. react to, greet, respond to, look forward to
6. free, light-hearted, humourous, frivolous
7. illegal, critical, prohibited, banned

He pulled out his mobile phone and called Sally Fielding. "Sally, Kevin here. Could you call Mike Patton and ask him about a break-in at P-Ride last night? Get whatever information you can from him, okay?" Mike Patton was a contact in the police that Blood and Flowers used frequently.
"No problem, Kevin. I'll get onto it right away."
"Thanks, Sally."

Chapter 7: Swimming with the Sharks

Blood walked into the office of a computer software company. The desks were piled up with papers and disks and coffee cups. The walls looked dirty and the floor too. IT companies have a reputation for being unique, but it appeared as if success had not yet visited this office. A woman in her mid-twenties looked up from the computer screen.

"If you're here about hardware problems, you're in the wrong place. Two doors down, you'll find what you're looking for."

"Actually," Blood said, "I'm here for Robin Watts."

Flowers had suggested that Blood visit this young man as he had helped Flowers a couple of times in the past six months. Blood was reluctant to ask him for help but now had no choice: neither he nor Flowers knew another computer hacker. A young man who had been hidden by the mess on the desks stood up and looked at Blood. Though his curly hair was a bit shorter, Blood still recognised him. They had met each other four years earlier – and not under the best of circumstances. Blood had been the arresting officer and had thus been required to speak at his trial. He walked up to Blood and held out his hand.

Übung 62: Bilden Sie die erste Steigerungsform der Adjektive!

1. short ____________________

2. successful ____________________

3. messy ____________________

4. recognisable ____________________

5. profitable ____________________

6. dirty ____________________

7. rich ____________________

8. practical ____________________

"I'm Robin Watts."

"Blood, David Blood." The young man looked at Blood expectantly. "You don't remember me, do you?" Blood asked finally.

"No, I don't."

"The last time you saw me," Blood said, "I was wearing a policeman's uniform." The man examined Blood a little closer but still did not recognise him. "I spoke at your trial."

Suddenly a look of fear crossed his face and then one of anger. "I'm not doing anything illegal. I'm trying to start my own software company. You've got no reason to be coming around here and harassing me. This is strictly legal."

"Good. But I'm here about something else. Do you have somewhere here where we could speak alone?"

Watts looked at Blood for a moment, then said, "Come with me," and led Blood back through the desks to a small office where another computer was set up.

"Is this the boss' office?"

"I'm the boss."

"And you have one employee?"

"Two."

"How's business?"

"It could be better. It might be some day, if I can just get a few contracts. We made a small profit last year, but it was eaten up by overheads. Renting an office in London is expensive."

Übung 63: Setzen Sie die Sätze in die indirekte Rede!

1. I'm the boss. (he)

He said that he was the boss.

2. I work for myself. (she)

____

3. I spoke at the trial. (he)

____

4. I have two employees. (she)

____

5. How's business? (he)

____

6. It might be successful someday. (she)

____

7. You have no reason to harass me. (he)

____

"I'm no longer a bobby. I work with a friend as a detective."
"Well, you're moving up in the world," Watts said with light sarcasm.
"I'm here to ask you a favour."
"I'm in business, sir. I don't do favours anymore. We don't do charity work here."
"Who said anything about charity work?" Blood said. He pulled out a £100 note. "I need your help getting access to a network."

"And you think £100 is going to do that? I spent 8 months in prison."

"Rest and relaxation in a low-security prison. It looks to me as if you could use a bit of money and I'm offering you a very brief contract. I know it isn't particularly lucrative, but I'm offering you a chance to use your skills in a good cause."

"What do you need?"

"What I need is for you to gain access to the network at First Sea Oil. I want to locate any communications that have to do with Beyond 2050, the environmental group, and anything they might have planned."

ÜBUNG 64 !

Übung 64: Wie lauten die Sätze in der richtigen Reihenfolge?

1. strictly is legal this.

____

2. 28 married been I years have for.

____

3. meeting discussed the was at what?

____

4. longer at I'm a president no vice First Sea.

____

5. seen report you have the?

____

6. red please a of would glass I like wine.

____

7. information interest I some of you have for.

8. want I to you a offer chance.

Watts looked at Blood a moment, then at the £100 note still in his hand. “This isn’t a set up, is it?”
“I told you, I’m no longer a bobby and I need your help. As far as that goes, my position in this is as bad as yours.”
“I don’t think it’s very likely that an ex-bobby will go to jail.”
“It does happen occasionally,” Blood responded. “This is easy money for you,” he added.
Watts began to work. “You know,” he said to Blood, “getting into company networks is not as easy as it once was. Each has its own new and improved firewall. And I’m out of practice. I haven’t done this since I went to prison. Okay, we’re on their website.” Watts told Blood what he was doing as he did it – and within 20 minutes he had gained partial access to the network. “I’m surprised they haven’t noticed me, yet.”
“They can’t trace this, can they?”
“Are you crazy? I’m not thick. You only caught me last time because I made a stupid mistake.”
“That was an expensive lesson.”
“I’ll say,” Watts agreed.

Übung 65: Beantworten Sie die Fragen zum Text!

ÜBUNG 65 !

1. What does Mr Rath think Kevin Flowers’ name is?

2. What is the job title of the person who confirms the rumour of the Big 3 meeting?

3. Who hired Blood Flowers Detectives at the beginning of the story?

4. Does Mr Rath give Flowers a lot of information?

5. Why does Flowers record his interviews?

"Have you found anything?"
"Not so far. I'm only part of the way in, though. This company needs to hire me as a consultant. I could fill in a few of the holes in their firewall. Okay, we're in."
"Really?"
"Really. What do you want to look for? You have to be quick; we could be thrown out at any minute."
"Let's see if we can find anything about Beyond 2050 or Future Watch on their network."
"Which one?"
"Let's take Future Watch first, as they're the larger organisation. Any document that mentions them, but I would especially like to find something where First Sea tries to discredit Future Watch or Beyond 2050."
Watts went through directories for a while but then finally said, "This isn't going to work. This is going to take far too much time."

"Just keep looking a little while longer. Can you do a search?"
"Not the kind you can do on your own computer. I don't think there is anything on Future Watch in here."
"Try Beyond 2050."
"I've been looking for both the whole time. It doesn't appear as if they are very concerned with either of these groups."
"I'm sure they are. These groups have made trouble for them."
"Well, I can't find evidence."
"Just keep trying."

Übung 66: Unterstreichen Sie die richtige Alternative!

"Here's something. They (1.) mean/mention having to respond to charges from Future Watch – and Beyond 2050 is also mentioned…"
"Let me see," Blood said, running around (2.) behind/over Watts. "Interesting. Could you print that?"
Watts pressed a (3.) tablet/button and began printing. "I'll look around a bit more but I'm not sure how much longer I'll be on." A few minutes later, they were (4.) logged/thrown out of the system.
Blood went over and looked at the letter they'd printed. 'We need to communicate more aggressively,' it says. 'Could we (5.) attempt/try Golden Day?'
"If you want to. I'll see what I can do." He (6.) took/spent a few minutes trying to get onto their site. "This is a bit more complicated."
"Just do what you can."
He worked a bit longer and then said, "Okay, we're on. I wasn't sure I was going to manage it. Their system is much better than First Sea's. I think Golden Day has a real IT Department – *they* haven't

been (7.) outsourced/outsized. Just like First Sea, though, finding what you're looking for is more the proverbial needle in a haystack."

"As I said before, just do the best you can. You've already got the money."
"It's a bit funny, you paying me to do this, when you helped arrest me for it several years ago."
"I know. But this is in a good cause. This isn't about my own financial gain, and it isn't just hooligans wreaking havoc. It's about uncovering illegal activities on the part of an international oil company."
"If you say so," Watts answered. "I just don't want to go back to jail for this. I don't do this anymore, really."
"You don't seem to have forgotten how to do it."
"It's like riding a bike. You never forget how. It's also simply about guess-work and intuition. That's the real challenge of it all and that's why it's a bit addictive. I don't really like doing it anymore, because it's playing with fire and I've already been burned once."

ÜBUNG 67 !

Übung 67: Wie heißen das Simple Past und das Past Participle der folgenden Verben? Setzen Sie ein!

1. is ____________ ____________
2. know ____________ ____________
3. give ____________ ____________
4. forget ____________ ____________
5. run ____________ ____________

6. find ____________ ____________

7. ride ____________ ____________

8. do ____________ ____________

Flowers got back to the office mid-afternoon. "Has Mac called me back yet, Sally?"
"The phones have been quiet, Kevin."
"Okay, I'd better give him another call," Flowers said and walked into his office. "What about Mike Patton?"
"He wasn't at his desk."
"Well, keep trying, Sally. I want to know whatever he knows, okay?"
"I'll do my best."
A woman in a dark suit walked up to the door of the Blood Flowers office and looked at the writing on the door and then walked away.
"I thought we were about to get another client," Fielding said.
"What?" Flowers called in from his office.
"Nothing, I just thought we were about to get another client, that's all." She sat down at her desk. "But she walked away."
Feeling a hand on her shoulder, Fielding shrieked and stood and turned to face Flowers. "Don't surprise me like that," she protested.
Flowers ignored her for the moment, however. He was looking out of the window above Fielding's desk.
"Is she gone?"
"How should I know?"
"What did she look like?"
"She wasn't anything special," Fielding answered. "She was just wearing a blue suit."
"Trousers or skirt?"
"Trousers."

ÜBUNG 68 !

Übung 68: Lesen Sie weiter und unterstreichen Sie die acht falsch geschriebenen Wörter. Geben Sie die richtige Schreibweise an!

Flowers ran out into the rode but it was empty. There was absolutly no motion anywhere, no breeze blowing and not even insekts were moving yet, so he went back into the office.

"Damn! Was she dark-haired or lite-haired?"

"Kev, you can't tell that in thin light. Look," she pointed out into the street, "there's been shadow here all day long. But she wasn't blonde, if that's what you were hoping."

"I wish she had been a blonde," Flowers said and disappeered into his office.

"Your toast in women is changing, Kev," Fielding called after him.

1. ____________ 2. ____________ 3. ____________

4. ____________ 5. ____________ 6. ____________

7. ____________ 8. ____________

Chapter 8: An Unexpected Visitor

"Mac," Flowers said, "you didn't call me back."

"I've been busy, Kevin, but don't worry: you're right up there on the priority list with the Queen and the Chancellor of the Exchequer."

"What do you know about the investigation into Future Watch?"

"There seems to have been an anonymous tip that some of the environmental groups are bursting with money. And then I passed on what you had said about the group that hired you. Future Watch is the biggest and so probably that seemed the obvious choice. Smaller groups like Beyond 2050 are not such a great concern, but Future Watch has begun exerting a more powerful influence in Britain and on the continent."

"Actually, Mac, erm, Beyond 2050 is the group that hired us."

"Hmm. That's interesting. Do they have a large membership?"

"I don't know. I've only met the leader, Preston Stiles, and the office manager. In their office I think they have desks for about seven people."

"What did you think of Stiles?"

"Well, I only met him once, but he seems to be a good leader. He's a good speaker, too."

"You saw the news conference, then?"

"Yes, of course. Mac, would it be possible for me to do a little research on Beyond 2050? Could you provide me access to certain files?"

"Could you be more specific?"

"I'd like to see where they're getting *their* money from."

"Why?"

"Because something about them seems too good to be true. They came out of nowhere in only a few years."

"I'll have to get back to you on that."

Übung 69: Welche Wörter passen zusammen?

ÜBUNG 69 !

1. anonymous	☐ assistant
2. obvious	☐ manager
3. powerful	☐ director
4. office	☐ tip
5. personal	☐ influence
6. personnel	☐ choice

Once Flowers was off the phone, Fielding walked in but stood silently while Flowers wrote himself a note. "Do you have something, Sally?" he asked at last.

"Yes. I spoke with Mike and he said that the break-in did indeed take place. One security guard got three stitches on a finger, so his injuries were really quite mild."

"Rath made it seem as if there was a bit more. That injury might even have been self-inflicted if he tried to pummel one of the people on the stairs."

"Yes, it could be. The struggle took place between the fifth and sixth floors, so it appears as if they were almost exactly halfway up to the twelfth floor. There were no identification marks on the black clothes of the men who broke in and they were wearing ski masks; the only thing that's certain is that they were men – from the build but also their voices."

"Have they found anything unusual yet?"

"Not as far as Mike knew. He said he'd keep us posted but that we shouldn't expect much. If it really was two people from one of the environmental groups, he said, they would just disappear back into the woodwork never to be found again."

"Hmm," Flowers answered. "We simply do not appear to be able to make any headway on this case at all. There's enough information to know that something is going on somewhere but it never quite comes together."

"Perhaps you'll get a sign soon," Fielding said encouragingly.

ÜBUNG 70 !

Übung 70: Setzen Sie die fehlenden Präpositionen ein!

1. I'll look ______ this matter.

2. They were not making progress ______ their project.

3. Can you find anything _____ their website?

4. I do not want to go to jail _____ this.

5. My line of business? I'm _____ computers.

6. Did you hear _____ you colleague this morning?

7. Are you going to speak _____ the meeting?

Blood walked into the office a bit later.
"Hello, Sally," he said and walked past into Flowers' office.
"You get anything?" Blood asked.
"More than I expected. Rath is one of the people who represented P-Ride at the meeting of the Big 3 a week ago. *He* admitted nothing. He's a really challenging bloke. He'd be fun for a pint down at the Shakespeare's Head but as an adversary he was difficult. In any case," Flowers resumed with a steady voice, "his personal assistant basically admitted that the meeting took place. She may even have been at it."
"Wow," Blood said, "we're finally making headway."
"No, we're not. It's the wrong case. We're trying to find out what these companies are doing to Beyond 2050, but each time we get information about the Big 3. What were you doing?" Flowers wanted to know.
"I was at our friend Robin Watts' office," Blood answered, smiling at his boss.
"Oh, right. Did you find out anything?"
"He did a little computer hacking for me, but we also came up nil. First Oil had a memo where they said there was 'a need to combat Future Watch more aggressively' – but that might only mean in the media where some of the biggest battles are fought," Blood summarized the facts.

"Has Stiles paid us anything?" Flowers asked. "Sally," he called out, "has Preston Stiles paid us anything for our work so far?"
"I know that he paid the down-payment, but I'll have to check to see if he transferred the second instalment."
"Please let me know what you find out."
"Will do, boss."

ÜBUNG 71 !

Übung 71: Ordnen Sie den Verben das passende Wort zu und tragen Sie die richtige Ziffer ein!

1. take down	☐ understand
2. take after	☐ begin
3. take in	☐ note
4. take up	☐ resemble
5. take over	☐ hire
6. take off	☐ lift
7. take out	☐ launch
8. take on	☐ assume control

"Let's go for a drive, Dave. You know how my head clears up when I drive."
"I've never understood how driving through heavy traffic and sitting in traffic jams helps you think. I know many people who go for walks or go for a jog, but you're the only one who goes for a drive."
"I go 'cruising,'" Flowers corrected, standing up and walking out of the office.
They walked out to Fielding's desk and said they would not be gone long. Flowers' car was parked not far away in a spot specially reserved for their building. Both men kept their cars parked here, as there was little parking near their flats and both could take a short

ride on the tube to work.

As he pulled out into the street, Flowers said. "I don't know if there's really a case here at all."

"Stiles says there is."

"But the facts don't corroborate that. His own assistant didn't know anything about the frozen accounts, the virus was a minor issue and could just as well have been caused by surfing the internet. What was his third point?"

"The banner," Blood answered.

"Yes, the banner," Flowers said. "What happened with that?"

"I never got to the bottom of that. I can only say that the guards on duty didn't seem to have had anything to do with it. Wisacker was so pissed off at them that it seemed real on his part too, although I think he was hiding something – I just don't know what. When I found the Golden Day additives in the boxes, it led me in another direction, away from Beyond 2050 and to this Big 3 meeting."

"Naturally. Everything takes us back to that."

Übung 72: Lesen Sie weiter und setzen Sie die passenden Wörter in die Lücken ein!

(visit, out, threatening, investigate, mobile, average)

The door opened and a man of (1.) __________ height walked in. "I would like to speak to a brown-haired man who works here." The man's voice was not quite (2.) __________ but there was something in it that said his (3.) __________ was not a friendly one.

"Jimmy Rogers?"

"Is that his name? Isn't there a Blood or a Flowers here?"

"Neither of them is here at the moment," Sally answered standing up and covering her (4.) __________ phone with her hand.

"Where are they?"

"They're (5.) __________ ."

The man looked around. "Who hired them to (6.) __________ oil companies?"

"I don't know anything about who hires them," Fielding responded, "I just answer the phones here." She managed to unlock her mobile phone, which she was holding behind her back, and then she used the menu button to call Flowers who was programmed first.
"You don't have to answer the phones anymore," he yelled and so saying, he picked her phone up, ripped the cables out of the wall and threw the phone itself against the wall. When it didn't seem to break, he picked it up and smashed it against the top of her desk.
"What are you doing here?" she asked again. "Why are you destroying the office?"
"Now that is a good idea. I will destroy the office."
"Who sent *you* here?" she asked.
"You'd better watch out, ma'am, or I might forget to be polite."

! ÜBUNG 73

Übung 73: Welche Synonyme gehören zusammen? Setzen Sie die richtige Ziffer ein!

1. corroborate	☐ forceful
2. instalment	☐ counterpart
3. aggressive	☐ strange
4. adversary	☐ confirm

5. apparent	☐ costs
6. funny	☐ payment
7. propose	☐ profitable
8. lucrative	☐ obvious
9. overheads	☐ put forward

Flowers had answered his mobile phone and after calling out "Sally" a couple of times, simply listened in. Once he heard that something was going on he handed the phone to Blood. "Something is happening back at the office. Listen in while I get us back there as fast as I can."

He hit the brakes hard, made an illegal turn in the middle of the road and began driving back to the office as fast as traffic would allow. He stopped at red lights when he had to but drove through them if it was safe to do so.

"What's going on?" Flowers asked.

"He seems to be doing a bit of damage to our office. Does our insurance cover this?"

"Forget our insurance, can you hear Sally? Is she okay?"

"No, I don't hear her, so I think she must be just standing there and watching. I hope she's all right."

"Who hired you to investigate the oil companies?" Blood heard.

Übung 74: Unterstreichen Sie die richtige Alternative!

"He's (1.) requiring/inquiring who hired us," Blood passed on to Flowers.

"I guess one of us, or maybe both, must have stood a little too heavily on somebody's (2.) toes/fingers."

"Don't get us killed, Kev," Blood said as they (3.) overpassed/

passed a car and narrowly avoided a car coming in the opposite direction. "We can't help Sally if we're dead or bleeding in the middle of the road. And don't kill anybody else."
"I've (4.) driven/drove much faster on these roads."
"Me too. But I still want to (5.) become/turn 38 next month."
"Can you hear anything?" Flowers asked.
"Yes, he just asked which office was yours. She's not answering directly."
"Good job."
"She's not going to be able to hold him (6.) on/off forever."
"She doesn't have to, because we're almost there. We're going to take a (7.) shortpath/shortcut down this one-way street."
"Something just went smash. Sally's asking him what he has against telephones. Oops, he's just seen the (8.) mobile/handy, I think."

"Is that you, Blood or Flowers?" called a voice loudly through the phone. "Who's there?"
Flowers shook his head 'No'. They turned a corner and were going down the road that led to the road their office was on.
"Well, whoever you are, I'm looking for you."
"And we're coming for you," Flowers couldn't help saying – but he said it quietly.
A moment later the phone went dead.
"Another phone down," Blood said.
Flowers turned onto the road that led to their office, accelerating as he finished the turn and driving as fast as he could. He slowed the car, drove up on the pavement and parked right in front of the door to the office.
Then Flowers jumped out of the car and ran into the office following behind Blood.

Übung 75: Sind folgende Aussagen korrekt? Markieren Sie mit richtig ✔ oder falsch – !

1. Robin Watts finds a surplus of information for David Blood. ☐
2. Flowers is unaware that he has been followed back to the office. ☐
3. Flowers is low on Mac's priority list. ☐
4. Stiles is thought to be a good speaker. ☐
5. Mac offers to provide Flowers access to all the information he wants. ☐
6. Blood and Flowers have absolute faith in Stiles. ☐
7. Sally Fielding denies knowing who hired Blood and Flowers. ☐

"Here you are," the man said, looking at Blood, "only you aren't him. Oh, there you are," he added, seeing Flowers enter, "now I was really hoping to meet you."
"The pleasure is all yours," Flowers responded.
The man made a lunge at Flowers who stepped to one side and tried to push him to the floor. He grabbed hold of Flowers' arm and tried to hit him. Instead, Flowers landed a blow. Blood ran over to Fielding who was simply standing against the wall watching everything.
"Who sent you?" Flowers asked as the man fell back a couple steps.
"That's what I came to find out from you," he answered and threw a fist at Flowers that hit home with a force Flowers had not quite expected.
Blood, seeing the blow land on Flowers' face, said, "Sally, go outside, get a safe distance away," and then tried to step between the two men, but was knocked to the ground by Flowers' adversary.
"I can handle him," Flowers yelled, "just get out of the way."
"We'll see what you can handle – Blood or Flowers or whatever your name is."

ÜBUNG 76

Übung 76: Setzen Sie die Sätze ins Perfekt!

1. I (live) here for ten years.

2. She (go) to Moscow.

3. David Blood (be) a detective for several years.

4. They (not give) a thought to the next project.

5. We (try) everything!

6. Your tickets (arrived, just).

7. (Be, ever) you to the headquarters?

Blood got up and ran outside and phoned the police. When he went back inside, both men were still at it. Flowers' nose was bleeding and the other man's lip was bleeding. One of the framed prints that Blood had brought to the office was lying on the floor in pieces. He looked around and saw that all the others were off the wall as well.
"Who hired you?" Flowers asked. "Did you get your orders from First Sea or from P-Ride?"
"Who hired you?" the other responded.

"The police are on their way," Blood announced.
The man answered with a blow to Flowers, which knocked him down, and then stepped over to Blood.
"Did I ask you to call the police?" he enquired and then hit Blood so hard that Blood fell to the floor like a stack of books.

Übung 77: Lesen Sie weiter und unterstreichen Sie die Synonyme der folgenden Wörter!
(1. interloper 2. pleased 3. response 4. chase 5. indicated 6. futile 7. misleading)

"I'm going to tell both of you right now," the intruder said, "we are not amused. We are going to find out who hired you, and we are going to make them pay a second time. You just let them know. We will find out. And you tell that little doll of a secretary that the next time I see her I'll use my charm to get an answer out of her."
Police sirens were in the air and the man ran out of the door and away. Flowers ran out in pursuit but stopped when he saw the police. He quickly described the man and pointed out the direction the man was headed, but he knew the search would be fruitless: the man was gone. His appearance was deceptive; he was far more powerful than he looked.

"Well," Fielding said, "if my job is going to be like this from now on, I need a pay rise."
"Are you okay?" Flowers asked, pressing his handkerchief against his bloody nose.
"I should ask you the same thing," she answered. Her face suddenly turned red, and she almost began to cry, but she regained control of herself and the moment passed.

"Sally, are you okay? He didn't touch you, did he?" Blood asked.

"He wasn't interested in me," Fielding answered.

"That's good," Blood said, relieved. "Wait, what do you mean he wasn't interested in you?" Blood asked with a small laugh.

"Not everybody looks at me the way you do, Dave," she said, shaking her head. Flowers laughed and Blood, despite himself, smiled.

"What are you two on about?" Fielding asked. "You wouldn't think that your office had just been turned upside-down."

"As long as you're okay, as long as nobody got hurt, or nobody got hurt badly, it's okay," Flowers whispered. "If anything had happened to you, I'd never have forgiven myself. Maybe we need to keep the office door locked from now on."

ÜBUNG 78 !

Übung 78: Setzen Sie die Aussagen ins Passiv!

1. Oil companies raise and lower their petrol prices.

____

2. Flowers drove recklessly.

____

3. The intruder destroyed the office.

____

4. I made the decision to invest in the struggling company six months ago.

____

5. Chile produces red and white wine.

____

6. People recognise that German automobiles are good quality.

Just then a policeman came in and reported that there was no sign of the suspect.

"Had you ever seen him before?"

They all said no, that he was a complete stranger, as far as they were concerned.

Blood, Flowers and Fielding all began answering a lot of questions, and after that they cleaned up the office.

"I need a new mobile phone, a new desk phone, a new computer screen and a pay rise," Fielding summarised as they locked the door for the day.

They walked her to her car and watched her drive away. As they walked together to the tube, each made sure that they were not being followed. They rode together to their local.

"Sally showed a lot of courage," Blood said and Flowers agreed, "we really should give her that pay rise." They were sitting over pints of bitter at the Shakespeare's Head.

"That guy could hit," Blood said. His cheek, right below his eye, was still tender.

"He must have been a boxer at one time," Flowers concluded, while touching his nose. "There was some real power behind his fists which I haven't felt since we left the police force."

"Most of the work we've done of late has been brain work," Blood said.

"Yes, it has. We're getting soft. We need to get in better shape," Flowers declared. "We need to start working out."

"Tomorrow," they said at the same time.

They had a few rounds and then went home.

ÜBUNG 79

Übung 79: Setzen Sie die passenden Fragewörter ein!

1. ___________ did the oil companies raise the prices by?
2. ___________ did the oil companies raise their prices?
3. ___________ does the oil come from?
4. ___________ company has the highest prices?
5. ___________ will prices go back down?
6. ___________ oil companies have headquarters in London?

"We have to decide what to do next," Flowers said, as they separated. "You noticed that the fellow said 'we', didn't you?"
"Yes, that was peculiar."
"Not if he meant the Big 3. I haven't been exactly subtle in my visits to P-Ride, First Oil or to Golden Day."
"I think I've done pretty well."
"You have, Dave," Flowers agreed, patting him on the back. "But today we got a message that we're moving into an area where the oil companies don't want us."
"As you keep saying, that isn't really where we're supposed to be looking anyway."
"No, it isn't," Flowers agreed, "though it seems that that is the place Preston Stiles wanted us to look. It'll all seem a little clearer in the morning, at least I hope it will. Good night."

Chapter 9: Picking up the Pieces

"It still doesn't look normal in here," Flowers said as he opened the door and walked in. "But I reckon that, unlike the old story of the shoemaker and the elves, the elves aren't going to do all the work for us."

"I just didn't want to go in alone," said Fielding, who had been waiting outside for him when he walked up. "I know no one is in there, but after yesterday it seems a bit different. I just couldn't go in."

"It's okay, Sally. We'll get things up and running and back in order again. In the meantime, we need to get our insurance agent here and get new phones."

"Well, one of you will have to lend me a mobile, as I don't have one any longer. I'll phone the insurance agent immediately, because they're going to pay for the new phones. It'll mean filling in a few forms and filing a claim."

"Do your best, Sally."

Übung 80: Lesen Sie weiter und setzen Sie die fehlenden Präpositionen ein!

Blood walked (1.) _____ carrying flowers. "After what you went through yesterday, Sally," he said, handing her the flowers, "I thought some flowers might brighten up the office (2.) _____ you."

"How thoughtful, Dave." She immediately put the flowers – orange tulips – (3.) _____ a vase.

Flowers walked up (4.) _____ Blood, just out (5.) _____ earshot (6.) _____ Fielding, and said, "You're getting a little close to the boundary, Dave."

"I looked (7.) _____ some perfume, but that's dangerous, too."

"Given what happened yesterday, I understand your motives – "
"It's okay, mate," Blood reassured him. "They're not roses."
"Just watch out, okay? So," Flowers said, changing the subject, "what do you think our next step is – besides refurbishing the office?"
"I don't suppose you could just go to First Sea or P-Ride and ask them why they sent that monster," Blood said.
"I think I should call Mac and let him know what has happened."
"That's a good first step."
"And then Preston Stiles and let him know."
"Yes, I could take care of that."
"I didn't mention this to you before, because I was still hoping that I was wrong, but I think I was followed back to the office after my 'interview' with Julian Rath at P-Ride. I think his personal assistant followed me back here – and that's how they figured out where to send our, uh, redecorator."
"How do you know she followed you? A blue suit is practically a uniform for women around here."
"I walked back to the office afterwards – it was finally a beautiful spring day. But it was stupid of me. She followed me out of the building and approached me to ask something – I answered and then I just walked away. It would have been so easy for her to follow me."

ÜBUNG 81 !

Übung 81: Welches Wort ist das „schwarze Schaf"? Unterstreichen Sie das nicht in die Reihe passende Wort!

1. accusation, charge, allegation, excuse
2. message, command, communique, note
3. refurbish, renovate, repeat, renew

4. representative, colleague, mediator, agent
5. assure, compel, require, oblige
6. erroneous, mistaken, phony, incorrect

"But how do you know she followed you?"
"Sally saw someone looking in the office door and it fitted her description. I ran out into the street when Sally said something but by that point she was gone. Besides, how else could they have found us here in London? It doesn't make sense."
"Can we turn that to our advantage somehow?" Blood asked.
"I don't see how, do you?"
"Tell Mac about P-Ride. Maybe he'd send somebody, or make a call or put a little pressure on them one way or another."
"I think," Flowers suggested, "we should also consider doing a brief investigation of Beyond 2050. I don't want to spend a lot of time on this – maybe just one morning, this morning, but I just want to be certain about them."
"Good idea," Blood agreed, "I'll visit Stiles."
"And I'll see if I can again access to their financial records."

Übung 82: Sind folgende Aussagen korrekt? Markieren Sie mit richtig ✔ oder falsch – !

ÜBUNG 82 !

1. Financial accounts tell you how to spend your money. ☐
2. Financial records contain lists of money coming and going out. ☐
3. Financial advisors tell you to spend your money. ☐
4. Financial directors decide how companies spend their money. ☐
5. Financial Departments employ accountants. ☐

"Petrol prices are still skyrocketing," Mac was saying over the phone. "I've never seen the like. I'm just waiting for the downward trend, but at the moment it looks like we're going to be driving under autumn leaves before that happens."

"Do you think it's price gouging?" Flowers asked.

"We haven't been asked to look into it," Mac answered.

"Yes, but *we* have."

"And have you found anything out?"

"We have no hard evidence, mainly denials. We have some hearsay and a partial admission that a meeting between the Big 3 took place."

"Hearsay won't do, Kev, you know that."

"I know, I know," Flowers conceded.

"And you mentioned a partial admission?"

"I caught the personal assistant to a senior executive at P-Ride off-guard when I asked her if she had been at the meeting," Flowers answered.

"And, what did she say?" Mac wanted to know.

"She started to ask me how I knew the meeting had taken place but then caught herself and refused to say anything further. But yesterday," Flowers continued, "we had a visitor from P-Ride, or someone working on behalf of the oil companies. He did a bit of redecorating – "

ÜBUNG 83 !

Übung 83: Kreuzen Sie die richtige Bedeutung der Sätze an!

1. He's as cool as a cucumber.
   a) ☐ He knows what he's doing.
   b) ☐ He's cold-hearted.
   c) ☐ He does not appear to react to pressure.

2. They spoke just out of earshot of the secretary.
   a) ☐ They made sure the secretary could not hear them.
   b) ☐ They made sure the secretary could hear them.
   c) ☐ They were angry with the secretary.

3. We're finally making headway.
   a) ☐ We have almost reached our destination.
   b) ☐ We are making progress.
   c) ☐ We have been waiting a long time.

4. You have to get to the bottom of this.
   a) ☐ You have to reach down there.
   b) ☐ You have to discover what is going on.
   c) ☐ You have to finish this project soon.

5. That's just hearsay!
   a) ☐ That's just a rumour.
   b) ☐ That's just something someone said.
   c) ☐ That's just repeating something I said.

6. Prices are skyrocketing.
   a) ☐ Prices are increasing.
   b) ☐ Prices are increasing quickly.
   c) ☐ Prices are exciting.

"What do you mean redecorating, Kevin?"
"Damage to our office – not to mention what he did to my face and Sally's nerves."
"Did something happen to Sally?"
"Not so much. The bloke didn't physically threaten her – but even just to watch whilst your office is systematically destroyed by some

thug is a bit stressful. You certainly don't feel safe simply because you're not a telephone or a computer."

"What makes you think he was from the oil companies?"

Flowers explained about being followed back to the office and mentioned the man using "we."

"You were careless, Flowers," Mac said.

"I know. I already feel bad enough about that. You don't have to rub it in."

"Of course I do, otherwise you'll never learn," he said with a brief laugh. "So, what do you want from me?"

"Bank records for Beyond 2050 and perhaps a little pressure on Julian Rath at P-Ride. I'm rather certain it was his personal assistant who followed me home."

"Bank records are already taken care of – I meant to phone you about that yesterday, right after I spoke to the Queen and the Prime Minister," he added ironically. "You know where to go. As for putting pressure on P-Ride, Kevin, I can't just run over there and walk in on them with nothing but what you've just told me."

"Why not?"

"That's not how we work here, you know that."

"That's how I work, though."

"And see where it's got you. Someone's gone and destroyed your office."

ÜBUNG 84 !

Übung 84: Ordnen Sie die Buchstaben zu einem sinnvollen Wort!

There was a moment of (1. ecilsen) __________ and then Mac continued, "I'll have to see what I can do. I'm not sure I can do anything at the (2. tonemm) __________." He asked Flowers to give him specific (3. seceip) __________ of information which he noted down.

They (4. guhn pu) __________ and Flowers went over to Fielding.

"What have you found out from the insurance people?"

"Since there's a police (5. trepor) __________, there's absolutely no problem. They already had a list of our office (6. tipquemne) __________, so that's taken care of. They're going to send a loss adjuster down this afternoon who has the clearance to (7. thirauseo) __________ payments. They asked if we wanted or needed business interruption – "

"Let's hope not," Flowers said.
"The only thing they said they wouldn't cover is my mobile phone," Fielding added.
"Naturally, we'll replace that," Flowers assured her. "You can go out over lunch and we'll reimburse you."
"Thanks, Kevin. We need three land-line phones and two computer screens. Your screen took a direct hit. David's monitor is still functioning, though it was also hit. A few prints are gone from the wall – and they'll be replaced, too."
"Perhaps we should just get a new monitor for Dave. It may just stop functioning tomorrow or the day after tomorrow, if it also received a hard whack."
"We're lucky we have the computer towers. They sit just out of sight on the floor."
"He must never have worked in an office," Flowers remarked.

"He certainly didn't look the type for office work," Fielding agreed.

ÜBUNG 85

Übung 85: Welche Gegenteile gehören zusammen? Ordnen Sie zu!

1. direct	☐ cautious
2. specific	☐ suppress
3. authorise	☐ general
4. careless	☐ produce
5. mention	☐ circuitous
6. destroy	☐ plummet
7. skyrocket	☐ prohibit

"I'm going out for a while to do some background research on Beyond 2050," Flowers said. "If I find out anything interesting, I'll give you a call."

"You can't call me," Blood said, "Sally is going to use my phone for the office."

"Okay, well, I'll be back in a couple of hours or so. Leave the door locked," Flowers called out.

"Good idea," Blood answered.

Flowers was admitted to a secured area where he was able to look at monthly bank statements for Beyond 2050 for the current year and two years past. Some of the deposits could be assumed to be membership fees, but when he came to the largest one, which was £525,000, he became suspicious. Where did this deposit come from? It was identified, in the statement, as XNT, but what was XNT? What did the letters stand for? Flowers looked over statements from the previous two years and – no surprise – found that XNT had made several similar deposits, though of varying amounts, in those years as well. Flowers made notes and then left for an archive in a London library where he could research organisations in the United Kingdom and around the world.

Übung 86: Beantworten Sie die Fragen zum Text!

ÜBUNG 86

1. What does Sally Fielding ask for after the intruder disappears?

____

2. What pieces of office equipment does the intruder dislike in particular?

____

3. Is Mac, at Scotland Yard, willing to jump in and help Flowers?

____

4. What is the job title of the person who settles insurance cases?

____

5. What is another word for screen?

____

6. What kind of records does Flowers want to look at?

____

David Blood meanwhile decided to pay Beyond 2050 another personal visit sooner rather than later. A telephone call would have sufficed, but he decided that he wanted to see just how busy the office was on a normal day, one where the people who usually worked there were not at a news conference. He was very cautious on his way to the office, however, making sure he was not being followed, and taking an indirect route that wound around London to the Beyond 2050 office, taking him through an area that was not busy and where any pursuer would be noticed. Certain that he was not being followed he made his way, at last, to the office building and pressed the buzzer.

Though it was a Thursday, the building seemed empty. A young man had answered the buzzer for Beyond 2050 and immediately let him in, but nobody was walking in the corridors on the ground floor. All the busy bees humming away at their desks, Blood thought. He took the lift to the top floor, once again saw the glass doors with Beyond 2050 written across them and, as before, saw the face of Justin Rhyes-Davies staring through them.

ÜBUNG 87 !

Übung 87: Lesen Sie weiter und unterstreichen Sie die acht falsch geschriebenen Wörter. Geben Sie die richtige Schreibweise an!

"What a surprize, Mr Blood," he said.

"Hello there," Blood respunded. "Is Mr Stiles in?" Blood looked around and saw that there were three other employers in the office, all on the phone and working at computers. Perhaps they're rec-rooting members, he thought.

"He is. Come right this way." Rhyes-Davies lead Blood towards the large office with glass windows, behind which the familar face of Preston Stiles was visible, looking at a computer screen.

"What are your colleges working on?" Blood asked.

"They're invoved in the campaign to lower petrol prices."

1. ______________ 2. ______________ 3. ______________

4. ____________ 5. ____________ 6. ____________

7. ____________ 8. ____________

"I thought you would be trying to reduce oil dependence altogether," Blood responded.
"Yes, we would like to, but we are also a consumer group, not merely an environmental group. Mr Blood here for you," Rhyes-Davies called as they came to the threshold of Stiles' office.
"Hello, Mr Blood," Stiles said quickly, "do you have something new to report?"
"I do, but it doesn't have anything directly to do with results of our case," Blood answered. Rhyes-Davies acted as if he were going to retreat to his desk, but Blood stopped him. "As you're the office manager," he said, "you might want to listen, too."

Übung 88: Welche Wörter gehören zusammen? Setzen Sie die richtige Ziffer ein!

ÜBUNG 88

1. damage	☐ fees
2. bank	☐ sheets
3. membership	☐ control
4. background	☐ options
5. balance	☐ statement
6. stock	☐ research

"What's up?" Stiles asked, looking a bit more concerned now.
"I thought you should know," Blood explained, "that we had a visitor yesterday, who partially destroyed our office."
"Oh, my word," Stiles exclaimed. "Nobody was injured, I hope."

"No, nobody was injured but a few things were destroyed in the office. The fellow simply entered the office and started breaking things. We fought him and managed to hold him off from doing too much damage. But, before he left, he said: 'We are not amused,' and then said that 'we' – whoever this *we* is – 'are going to find out who hired you.' I made sure that I wasn't being followed before I came here, but I thought I should warn you that you, too, might potentially be at some risk. The young man who came to our office yesterday was surprisingly strong and moderately destructive. Naturally we did not reveal that you hired us."

"I should think," Stiles complained, but managing to still sound concerned, "that a phone call would have been sufficient to tell us this news."

"Perhaps. But considering the gravity of the situation, I thought a personal visit might be in order. Perhaps we should discuss any possible courses of action if your office were to be similarly attacked."

ÜBUNG 89 !

Übung 89: Unterstreichen Sie die richtige Alternative!

"I think that's quite (1.) unnecessary/unlikely," Stiles objected, "especially since you were not followed here. We have nothing of (2.) price/value here and the office equipment is all covered by insurance."

"Okay. So," Blood said, changing the (3.) subject/theme, "have you been quite busy since your news conference the other day?"

"Yes, we have, Mr Blood, we want to (4.) coordinate/organise our efforts with some of the other organisations (5.) joining/present at the conference and find ourselves snowed under at the moment. Working with other groups always seems to (6.) evolve/involve

more work rather than less. Look, Mr Blood, considering what just happened to your (7.) house/office, perhaps I should pay you the final instalment in advance. It seems that you are making the right people unhappy with your investigation and so your (8.) works/efforts should be rewarded."
"Thank you," Blood said – and soon (9.) thereafter/thereby left the Beyond 2050 office.

Chapter 10: Sifting through the Dirt

At the same time, Flowers was at the British Library going through the business archive to determine who XNT was. Once he had located the correct book, for the current year, he went through the X section but found nothing that went with XNT. He came up with medical, patient and even traffic organisations, foundations, committees but nothing with the right initials.
He sat back in his chair and looked up at the ceiling. The wall sconces lit the room rather poorly and threw round shadows on the ceiling. Suddenly a shadow moved across the ceiling and Flowers thought of the Tube and then his mind wandered to his visit to Chicago several years earlier and the elevated train that circled around and through the city centre and then extended north and south of the city. The elevated, he thought, was called 'the L' for short. El becomes L. X is ex as well. I could also look in E's, Flowers realised, in the Ex's even. The thick section of E's was considerably shortened by focusing on the Ex's – and within minutes Flowers had found Extra Neutral Technology. That sounds like a good foundation for a company with environmental concerns, Flowers thought. Find some energy source that is neutral, that isn't harmful to the environment, and exploit it.

ÜBUNG 90 !

Übung 90: Haben die Wörter dieselbe Bedeutung? Markieren Sie richtig ✔ oder falsch – !

1. information/news ☐
2. identify/compare ☐
3. basic/cardinal ☐
4. assistant/subordinate ☐
5. desk/bar ☐
6. accelerate/increase ☐
7. force/push ☐

Still, Flowers continued, I should be thorough and do a little background research on the organisation to make sure that it, too, is legitimate. He wrote down the names of the director and the members of the board of directors and then went to a library computer and got on the internet. The first search, on Thomas Strangeways, the director of the organisation, came up a winner. He also happened to be on the board of directors for Ipsopax, a British oil company that only *sounded* as if it came from Greece. This company was the Number 4 oil company in the UK. A quick search for the members of the board of directors revealed that two of them were members of international financial institutions, while a third was in senior management at Ipsopax. They make a very solid team of pro-environmental supporters, Flowers said to himself. It's also clear why Stiles is focusing on the Big 3 – they're the competition. Flowers wrote himself some notes and then left the library. Outside he phoned the office, using Blood's mobile number.

ÜBUNG 91 !

Übung 91: Setzen Sie die Wörter in Klammern richtig ein!
(board of directors, chief information officer, middle management, chief executive officer, senior management, work force)

1. People employed at a company are its __________.

2. A person hired to direct a company is the __________.

3. People who manage employees directly are usually in ________.

4. People who manage the managers are generally in __________.

5. A group of people with ultimate responsibility for the direction of a company is its __________.

6. A person who is responsible for the public "face" of the company is the __________.

"Hello, Kevin," Fielding answered, "what's up?"
"Hello, Sally," Flowers answered. "Is Dave there?"
"No, I'm on my own at the moment – with the door still locked," Fielding explained.
"Good. As soon as Dave gets back, tell him that Beyond 2050 receive most of their financial support from Ipsopax."
"From Ipsopax!" Fielding exclaimed. "What? That man is a fraud?"
"I'm not sure what Stiles is," Flowers replied, "but he's playing a dirty game with us."
"That makes me boiling mad," she said.
"Just don't forget to tell Dave as soon as you see him."
"You'd better believe I won't," she said, still sounding offended.

Flowers hung up the phone and decided that he would make the rounds of the boxing gyms in London to see if he could discover the identity of the attacker from the previous day. The first was not too far from the library, maybe half a mile or so away.
"He was about five foot seven, with short dark hair. He didn't look strong at all but he had power."

ÜBUNG 92

!

Übung 92: Lesen Sie weiter und fügen Sie die richtigen Präpositionen ein!

Managers (1.) _____ several (2.) _____ the gyms knew no one who met such a description. One, however, said that the description might be (3.) _____ a certain well-known local wrestler.

"You know, that fake wrestling (4.) _____ telly. They all have these stage names and throw each other around the ring. Some (5.) _____ them wear masks. Well, there's this one fellow who looks as (6.) _____ he won't last a minute (7.) _____ the ring but manages (8.) _____ put down some pretty strong men."

"That sounds familiar," Flowers said.
"The guys who do this are often fat and not very strong for their size, but some of them were boxers in the past and still work out today. This one that I'm talking about is known as Gentleman Jim. He wears a black rubber mask, so I don't know what he looks like, but he might be your man."

The manager told Flowers where he could find the gym where such athletes worked out and Flowers paid that gym a visit.
The manager there had photographs of all the boxers and wrestlers who regularly trained in his gym. Gentleman Jim, known to his mother as Randy Tuey, was without a doubt the fellow who had 'redecorated' the Blood Flowers office.
"Come back around 2pm," the manager said. "He usually comes in around then."
"Thanks, I'll be there."

Übung 93: Wie heißt das Wort auf Deutsch?

1. fake	☐ Sporthalle	4. library	☐ trainieren
2. wrestling	☐ Betrug	5. fraud	☐ Ringen
3. gymnasium	☐ vortäuschen	6. work out	☐ Bibliothek

Flowers had an hour to wait so he went to a café and ordered a cup of tea. He thought about what he was going to do and say. It was certain that Randy Tuey was going to be surrounded by friends and colleagues. The first thing he had to do then was make it clear that he was not threatening – but could be if necessary. All he really wanted to know was who had hired him. Shortly after 2pm, Flowers strolled back to the gym. The manager pointed out the area where Tuey was lifting weights. The young man did not notice Flowers until he was standing right in front of him.

"You – how did you find me?"

"You're not a professional at this, are you?" Flowers asked.

"Well, what are you doing here?" he asked, making no move to escape.

"I came to talk."

"Well, I'm not in the mood to talk."

"That would be a mistake."

"It would, would it?"

"Yes. I have some Scotland Yard colleagues," Flowers said, holding up his mobile phone, "who are interested in what you have to say and what you don't have to say."

"Look around you. These people will help me if I call on them."

"You can ask them right now just how many of them are ready to go to jail for you. Go on, ask them." Flowers looked the young man right in the eyes until the other looked away.

"What do you want?" he asked finally.

"Now, I don't particularly care about what you did yesterday. I have insurance which will pay for the damage. What I do care about, however, is who hired you. I know it wasn't personal – I've never seen you before and neither had my colleagues. So, who hired you?"

ÜBUNG 94 !

Übung 94: Welches Wort ist das „schwarze Schaf"?

1. fake, freak, counterfeit, phony
2. intention, interest, curiousity, attention
3. mood, disposition, mad, humour
4. encircle, envelop, surround, enhance
5. changling, charlatan, fraud, cheat
6. section, segment, part, particle

"Well, I don't know who it was. Someone just gave me £500 to give you a message."
"Randy, prison has been known to work wonders on the memory. Naturally, you wouldn't be in for very long, if at all. Maybe only this afternoon, but once you're caught up in the system it can seem like forever. Let me ask you the question once more, who hired you?"
"It was just some bloke who came in and asked me if I might be willing to help him with a problem."
"And this fellow was about sixty, bleached blond hair?"
"Not at all. He was mid-twenties, a little younger than me, and sort of a mousy type wearing a suit. He seemed just scared to be here."
"No name?"
"What do I need a name for? His name was £500. That's good enough for me. How about you?"

"I might need more. Tell me exactly what he wanted you to do."
"Just scare you a little. He said I should smash things up a bit."
"And you did that without any name from him? You took all the risk yourself? That's really very bright."
"He first offered me £200 and after a bit of discussion when I agreed not to ask for any information we agreed on £500. I call that good bargaining. And I didn't really hurt you. I just gave you a workout. You should watch me on television and see what I can do."
"It's all fake, Randy."
"Only *some* of it's fake."

Übung 95: Welche Wörter gehören in die Lücken?
(reported, described, instalment, discovered, funded, brought, found, respective, discussed)

Blood and Flowers (1.) __________ their (2.) __________ mornings and (3.) __________ the news, Blood speaking first. "Sally," said Flowers, "would you check on Blood's computer if we've been paid the final (4.) __________ from Beyond 2050?" Then Flowers (5.) __________ on his morning and early afternoon. Blood had already (6.) __________ out from Fielding that Beyond 2050 was (7.) __________ by Ipsopax but wanted the details of how Flowers (8.) __________ this piece of news. Then Flowers (9.) __________ him up to date with the visit to the gym.

"He said it was a mousy type who hired him to visit us," Flowers said to Blood, "who do we know who's mousy?"

"That Justin Rhyes-Davies. Remember him looking through the windows at Beyond 2050."
"You're absolutely right," Flowers said.
"We should go and visit him right now and give him a punching-up of his own."
"Dave. We have to be subtle here. We have to find out why Stiles hired us. Was it simply to put pressure on the Big 3 or is something else going on?"
"I think we should bring Mac up to speed on this," Blood declared.
"I agree. Later. Sally? Is the money in?"
"Yes, it is."

! ÜBUNG 96

Übung 96: Setzen Sie, wenn nötig, den bestimmten oder unbestimmten Artikel ein!

1. Flowers went to ______ library.

2. While waiting, he went to ______ café.

3. She spent two years at ______ university.

4. ______ May is a beautiful month.

5. That was ______ first time it ever happened to me.

6. I haven't been there for ______ years.

7. Let's go for ______ ride.

"First we speak with Stiles," Flowers announced. "Then we speak with Mac. No mention yet about Gentleman Jim, okay? We don't want to reveal everything we know all at once."
They drove over to Beyond 2050 and stood outside for a few minutes

waiting for someone to come out. They did not want to alert Stiles or Rhyes-Davies that they were going to be visited. After twenty minutes, Flowers was growing impatient. "Time for the happy idiot." He pressed on the buzzer of a company on the first floor.
"Yes?"
"Delivery," Flowers said in his put-on accent.
"Did we order anything?"
"That's why I'm here."
There was a discussion in the background and then a voice said, "We didn't order anything."
"Right you are," Flowers agreed, "and yet I'm here with something for you or someone in this building." The buzzer sounded and in walked Flowers and Blood. "Let's take the stairs," he said in his normal voice.
They made their way to the third floor and entered the Beyond 2050 office unannounced.

Übung 97: Lesen Sie weiter und setzen Sie die Verben in der richtigen Zeitform ein!

Rhyes-Davies (1. stand) __________ up. "What?" he asked. Blood (2. wink) __________ at him and followed Flowers to Stiles' office. They (3. can) __________ see him sitting in his office and the look of surprise and dismay that crossed his face. He (4. get) __________ up and walked around from behind his desk.

"What (5. bring) __________ you here?" he asked, clearly baffled by their presence.

"We just have a couple of questions," Flowers said. "Like, what (6. be) – __________ your relationship to XNT and what (7. be) __________ XNT's relationship to – Ipsopax?"

"Just because there's a relationship doesn't mean that they have any influence on our politics or our activities," Stiles declared.
"You don't believe that and we don't believe that either," Flowers responded.
"Yeah, come on, mate," Blood said, "just tell us what the game is."
"There is no game," Stiles said warmly, "we are a legitimate organisation."
"No doubt. But," Flowers added, "legitimacy is always a question of perspective. Legitimate in whose eyes? Legally, sure you're legitimate; but to the people who are your members, if there really are any members, and to people who support and work for Future Watch and other organisations – I doubt your group will be legitimate any more. The real game was that you wanted us to help you make the Big 3 look bad. That's all we were ever supposed to do, help you and Scotland Yard throw mud at the Big 3."
"And they're an easy target because they're so greedy," Blood added. "In the end," Flowers continued, "it was all just to help increase sales for Ipsopax and nothing more."
"Even if you expose our financial sources," Stiles argued, ignoring Flowers' accusation, "we have managed to focus attention on the Big 3, who *are* doing the most damage, and that was *always* our only goal."
Flowers and Blood walked out of the office, back down the stairs and to Flowers' car.
"You have to admire him," Blood said, "he's a real fighter. He may go down, but he goes down swinging."

Übung 98: Haben die Wörter oder Phrasen dieselbe Bedeutung? Markieren Sie richtig ✔ oder falsch – !

1. wink/wave ☐
2. stairs/steps ☐
3. meet somebody/see somebody ☐
4. order/directive ☐
5. impatient/tired ☐
6. date with a lawyer/appointment with a lawyer ☐
7. post/job ☐
8. legitimate/legal ☐
9. spell out/make clear ☐
10. beyond doubt/beyond question ☐

Back at the office, a loss adjuster was speaking with Sally Fielding.
"Everything's in order," the man said.
"I've ordered the new equipment and it will be delivered tomorrow."
"We've made sure that the telephone people will be here tomorrow, too. The damage is minimal but we don't want there to be any disruption in your business."
"Thank you for your help," Blood said.

Flowers called Mac.
"So, how many times are you going to call me today? My own wife doesn't call as often as you do."
Flowers reported everything that had gone on in what had become a very eventful day.
"Well, that paints everything in a very different light. That certainly demands further investigation."
"I thought you might see it that way."

Übung 99: Markieren Sie mit richtig ✔ oder falsch – !

1. Randy Tuey denies he damaged anything in Flowers' office. ☐
2. Tuey says the person who hired him was named £500. ☐
3. Preston Stiles denies that Beyond 2050 is funded by an oil company. ☐
4. Stiles is surprised by Flowers' and Blood's final visit. ☐
5. Blood thinks Stiles is a weakling. ☐
6. Flowers accuses Stiles of being a fraud. ☐
7. Stiles defends his organisation. ☐

Two days later the newspapers were full of the report that the government was going to investigate Beyond 2050 and Ipsopax – as well as the Big 3. "There is a lot of uncertainty now about all the activities of the oil companies. There appear to have been illegal activities on all sides. We will get to the bottom of this," the government's communique promised.

"There's a Preston Stiles on the phone for you," Fielding said ironically, putting a call through to Flowers.

"Flowers here, what can I do for you, Mr Stiles?"

"We want our fees returned straight away. Your report to the press has made difficulties not only for us but for our supporting foundation. I never authorised you to go to the press with the information that we *paid you* to recover. It was our information, for our use: not for you to disseminate."

"But Mr Stiles. We didn't speak to the press. We only spoke to our contact at Scotland Yard just as you asked us to. I was only following your orders. Considering that, I think there are no grounds for refunding your money."

The phone at the other end was slammed down hard.

"Another satisfied customer," Flowers called out.

"What?" Blood asked, walking into the office.
"That was Stiles on the phone. He wants his money back."
"You're not going to give it back to him, are you?"
"No, *we're* not. But I wonder if this whole business is going to be good or bad for our reputation."
"Our job," said Blood, "is always to get at the truth and we did, didn't we?"

Übung 100: Welche Wörter haben eine ähnliche Bedeutung? Ordnen Sie zu!

ÜBUNG 100 !

1. contact	☐ call for
2. disseminate	☐ statement
3. recover	☐ institution
4. foundation	☐ connection
5. communique	☐ circulate
6. demand	☐ distributor
7. supplier	☐ recoup

Nine months later, after much investigation and a court trial, it came out that the meeting of the Big 3 did take place. However, the meeting was to discuss a threat facing the companies: they were being forced to raise their prices because Ipsopax was forcing a supplier to raise its prices with threats to unveil other illegal activities by the Big 3. Naturally, Ipsopax had raised their prices too but it was pure profit.

THE END

Abschlusstest

Übung 1: Welches Wort ist das „schwarze Schaf"?

1. post, firm, company, business
2. curiousity, interest, intervention, attention
3. boss, manager, secretary, director
4. limitless, limitation, weakness, disadvantage
5. oblige, assure, compel, require
6. duplicate, copy, reproduction, report
7. charges, income, expenses, costs

Übung 2: Welche Wörter gehören in die Lücken?
(discredit, raising, frozen, book, secured, enquiring, fluctuations, reliance)

1. "That Sunday night flight was the only one I could __________."
2. "We want to see less ___________ on animal products."
3. "Everyone else is ___________ prices, why don't we?"
4. He described ___________ in the price of crude oil.
5. The environmental groups want to __________ the oil companies.
6. Stiles said the accounts were ___________.
7. "He's __________ about who hired us."
8. Flowers was admitted to a ___________ area.

Übung 3: Unterstreichen Sie die richtige Alternative!

1. We are for a clean environment and investment/involvement in renewable energy sources.
2. We have the promise of a benefit/bonus if we get the proof he wants.
3. Were there no signs of forced entry/admission?
4. I meant/mentioned finding a letter on my desk.
5. I still want to become/turn 38 next month.
6. Blood changed the subject/theme.

Übung 4: Welche Synonyme gehören zusammen? Setzen Sie die richtige Ziffer ein!

1. successful	☐ employees
2. explode	☐ engagement
3. appropriate	☐ strange
4. total business	☐ flourishing
5. appointment	☐ skyrocket
6. staff	☐ turnover
7. funny	☐ lucrative
8. profitable	☐ suitable

Übung 5: Setzen Sie die Wörter zu einem sinnvollen Satz zusammen!

1. much was secretary Fielding than a Sally more

____

2. are detectives missing retrieve hired persons to

____

3. monthly finished report you have the?

___

4. member is a the of legal solicitor profession a

___

5. man Blood the crime asked scene young the him to to escort

___

6. personal longer at I'm assistant no First Sea.

___

7. him, okay from whatever get you can information?

___

Übung 6: Welche Präpositionen gehören in die Lücken?

1. You will be ________ trouble.
2. An assistant is used to being the bearer ________ bad news.
3. Who was ________ duty yesterday?
4. She was ______ her late 20s.
5. I'll have to look ______ this matter.
6. What's your line of business? I'm ______ marketing.
7. Have you heard ______ Ms Fielding today?
8. I was looking ______ it everywhere, but couldn't find it.
9. He finally left the house ______ six ______ the evening.

Übung 7: Welche Verben und Substantive gehören zusammen? Kreuzen Sie an!

1. receive	☐ efforts
2. personnel	☐ records
3. balance	☐ meetings
4. senior	☐ orientation
5. financial	☐ manager
6. coordinate	☐ property
7. personal	☐ management
8. customer	☐ sheet
9. attend	☐ mail

Übung 8: Übersetzen Sie die folgenden Begriffe ins Englische!

1. dienstlich ______________
2. Untersuchung ______________
3. Vermögenswerte ______________
4. überzeugen ______________
5. überbringen ______________
6. Betreffzeile ______________
7. dringend ______________
8. Aktentasche ______________
9. teilnehmen ______________
10. Besucherparkplatz ______________

Übung 9: Formulieren Sie die Sätze in der indirekten Rede!

1. "I am very tired," she said.

2. "It has been a very interesting day," they said.

3. "I am always talking to myself," she said.

4. "We will be at the meeting on time," he said.

5. "Have you got any money?" she asked.

6. "Let's go to the Indian restaurant," she suggested.

7. "I cannot change the appointment," he said.

8. "I worked twelve hours yesterday," he said.

Lösungen

Übung 1: 1. comment 2. organisation 3. investigation 4. rising 5. usually 6. complaint 7. profession 8. prices Lösung: consumer
Übung 2: 1. office 2. clients 3. month 4. time 5. holiday 6. Justice 7. work 8. flight 9. discretion
Übung 3: 1. Sally Fielding was (quickly) checking the post quickly. 2. Fielding was more than a secretary. 3. Fielding worked as personal assistant and office manager for Flowers and Blood 4. Detectives retrieve missing people 5. Absolute discretion was one of Sally Fielding's qualities.
Übung 4: 1. holiday 2. patient 3. post 4. secretary 5. exercise 6. income
Übung 5: 1. - 2. - 3. ✔ 4. - 5. - 6. -
Übung 6: 1. interviewer 2. changed 3. investment 4. reliance 5. uneconomical 6. successful 7. confident
Übung 7: 1. Companies should invest in renewable energies. 2. Preston Stiles is the director of an environmental and consumer advocate organisation. 3. The computer network is infected with a virus. 4. Oil companies are disrupting the activities of Beyond 2050. 5. Criminals have frozen the financial assets.
Übung 8: 1. Die Preise schnellen in die Höhe. 2. ein wenig Überzeugungsarbeit leisten 3. den Weg in die Nachrichten finden 4. etwas zum Thema machen 5. eine Absprache zwischen Firmen 6. Das ist schwer zu beweisen. 7. ein Verbrechen begehen
Übung 9: 1. firm 2. efficient 3. flourishing 4. executive 5. fee 6. to explode 7. appointment 8. authorised 9. to accept
Übung 10: 1. meeting 2. strategies 3. action plan 4. companies 5. CEOs 6. boards of directors 7. senior managers 8. subsidiaries 9. competitors 10. oil prices 11. tax increases 12. prices
Übung 11: 1. raising 2. downward 3. next step 4. deliver 5. fake 6. credit cards 7. business cards 8. successfully 9. cases 10. fair 11. labour
Übung 12: 1. a 2. a 3. a 4. b 5. b
Übung 13: 1. for 2. up 3. to 4. about 5. in 6. for 7. of 8. about 9. into 10. about 11. of 12. up
Übung 14: 1. He wants to deliver a letter for Mr. Pomeroy. 2. The letter was very official-looking. 3. The legal document has to be signed by Mr. Pomeroy personally. 4. He dialled Mr. Pomeroy's number on his mobile phone. 5. Can I see your identification?
Übung 15: 1. personal assistant 2. purchasing department 3. visitor's pass 4. confirmed 5. colleagues 6. security
Übung 16: 1. desk diary 2. meeting 3. desk 4. top management 5. briefcase 6. electronic organiser 7. scrolled back 8. date 9. CEO

Übung 17: 1. (computer) mouse 2. email account 3. password 4. subject line 5. USB stick 6. file 7. directory
Übung 18: 1. to receive 2. to sign 3. to page 4. to note 5. to explain 6. to access 7. to suspect 8. to copy
Übung 19: 1. reception 2. office 3. sign 4. personal assistant 5. urgent 6. visitor's pass 7. document 8. counter 9. briefcase
Übung 20: 1. Flowers was examining the CEO's desk and computer. 2. The detective needed the administrative assistant's signature. 3. Flowers handed her the legal document. 4. Flowers put the signed form back in his briefcase. 5. A solicitor is a member of the legal profession.
Übung 21: 1. document 2. attend 3. meeting 4. manipulate 5. organise 6. minutes 7. receipt 8. system Lösung: managers
Übung 22: 1. to attend a meeting 2. to follow an order 3. to pull the strings 4. to take a look 5. to copy a file 6. to abuse trust
Übung 23: 1. check-in 2. nearly 3. signature 4. computer. 5. arrangement 6. research 7. files 8. opportunity 9. ignore 10. come upon
Übung 24: 1. values 2. translate 3. raise 4. increases 5. profits 6. distributors 7. market 8. competing 9. turnover
Übung 25: 1. volume 2. merchant 3. to battle 4. example 5. suitable 6. to propose 7. purpose
Übung 26: 1. b 2. a 3. a 4. b 5. a 6. a
Übung 27: 1. fees 2. bonus 3. environmental 4. the point 5. raise 6. publicity 7. busy 8. updated
Übung 28: 1. Blood parked his car in the visitor's car park. 2. He went up to the security office. 3. The building was a typical prefabricated building. 4. Is it possible to speak to the plant manager? 5. I'm here on (official) business.
Übung 29: 1. expected 2. reported 3. matters 4. reports 5. produce 6. commercials 7. deliver 8. petrol stations 9. shopping
Übung 30: 1. Blood found out that Pomeroy wanted to put pressure on one of the distributors. 2. Blood wanted to discover if the banner was still there and who made it. 3. They called him 'Mac' because he worked at Scotland Yard and many last names in Scotland start with Mac or Mc. 4. John Glaser is Blood's undercover identity. 5. He found the banner.
Übung 31: 1. Maybe they wanted to have a little fun. 2. I've seen your signature on my business plan. 3. Then they started a little square dance. 4. And I think I'm going to apply for a job at this refinery. 5. Wisacker pulled out his electronic organiser. 6. I have forgotten the password of my computer. 7. One day I will be the CEO of one of the three big oil companies!
Übung 32: 1. a 2. a 3. b 4. a 5. b 6. a

Übung 33: 1. in front of 2. questions 3. high 4. bought 5. quickly 6. consumers 7. continued 8. fall 9. decrease
Übung 34: 1. crystal ball 2. subject 3. relationship 4. challenge 5. standard 6. competitor 7. rumour
Übung 35: 1. lift 2. gestured 3. company 4. guard 5. colleague 6. energy 7. careful
Übung 36: 1. to follow 2. office 3. transfer 4. to play 5. demonstration
Übung 37: 1. solved 2. guards 3. addresses 4. storage area 5. contain 6. delivered
Übung 38: 1. How late do you (usually) work, usually? 2. He gave him the telephone receiver. 3. Who is on duty this evening? 4. He got a company car from his employer. 5. The goods are in the storage area.
Übung 39: 1. to 2. on 3. to 4. up 5. at 6. on 7. at
Übung 40: 1. depends on 2. screen 3. management 4. deliveries 5. lorries 6. entry
Übung 41: The management told the security guards to focus on certain areas. 2. There were late deliveries the other night. 3. Everybody working at the plant had a set of keys. 4. No keys were reported missing. 5. Blood asked the young guard to escort him to the storage area.
Übung 42: 1. worked 2. job 3. entrance/door 4. examining 5. trucks 6. possibility/opportunity 7. documents
Übung 43: 1. compartment 2. order 3. instead 4. position 5. enter 6. duplicate 7. delivery 8. refinery Lösung: additive
Übung 44: 1. to have a secret 2. to nod his head 3. to shrug her/his shoulders 4. to get orders 5. to work long hours 6. to address a colleague 7. to employ a security guard 8. to monitor the plant
Übung 45: 1. industry 2. function(ality) 3. leader 4. government 5. investigation 6. perfection
Übung 46: 1. suspicions 2. products 3. desk 4. working 5. a press conference 6. leading 7. involved
Übung 47: 1. b 2. a 3. a 4. b 5. a
Übung 48: 1. ✔ 2. ✔ 3. - 4. - 5. ✔ 6. - 7. -
Übung 49: 1. to forward 2. to confirm 3. to explain 4. consumer 5. guarantee 6. to miss
Übung 50: 1. That's not what we were hired for! 2. We should focus/concentrate on our job! 3. I think we can handle this! 4. We'd like to be informed about the latest developments! 5. No one is monitoring the monitors/watching the watchers!
Übung 51: 1. buzzed 2. lift 3. branch 4. insurance 5. afford 6. glass doors
Übung 52: 1. full-time 2. (donor) member 3. accountant 4. volunteer 5. organiser 6. assistant 7. detective

Übung 53: 1. capital 2. money 3. earnings 4. duty 5. aim 6. accomplishment 7. scheme 8. study 9. origin
Übung 54: 1. passed 2. give 3. unfamiliar 4. around 5. in 6. leave 7. information 8. appointment
Übung 55: 1. engagement 2. elevator 3. credentials 4. permit 5. staff 6. desk clerk
Übung 56: 1. on 2. into 3. in 4. in 5. on 6. in 7. from
Übung 57: 1. a 2. c 3. b 4. a 5. c
Übung 58: 1. stunned 2. thought 3. cannot 4. would 5. Are you saying 6. were 7. Do you have
Übung 59: 1. staff 2. managers 3. trade 4. authorised 5. major 6. security
Übung 60: 1. strict 2. respect 3. distant 4. confusion 5. indifference 6. discriminatory
Übung 61: 1. confront 2. refute 3. reproduce 4. limitless 5. look forward to 6. free 7. critical
Übung 62: 1. shorter 2. more successful 3. messier 4. more recognisable 5. more profitable 6. dirtier 7. richer 8. more practical
Übung 63: 1. He said that he was the boss. 2. She said that she worked for herself. 3. He said that he had spoken at the trial. 4. She said that she had two employees. 5. He asked how business was. 6. She said that it might be successful someday. 7. He said that I had no reason to harass him. 8. I want to offer you a chance.
Übung 64: 1. This is strictly legal. 2. I have been married for 28 years. 3. What was discussed at the meeting? 4. I'm no longer a vice president at First Sea. 5. Have you seen the report? 6. I would like a glass of red wine please. 7. I have some information of interest for you.
Übung 65: 1. He thinks it is Jimmy Rogers. 2. The job title is personal assistant. 3. Preston Stiles hired Blood Flowers Detectives. 4. No, he does not. 5. He wants to appear to be a real journalist.
Übung 66: 1. mention 2. behind 3. button 4. thrown 5. try 6. spent 7. outsourced
Übung 67: 1. was, been 2. knew, known 3. gave, given 4. forgot, forgotten 5. ran, run 6. found, found 7. rode, ridden 8. did, done
Übung 68: 1. rode/road 2. absolutly/absolutely 3. insekts/insects 4. lite/light 5. thin/this 6. hear/here 7. disappeered/disappeared 8. toast/taste
Übung 69: 1. tip 2. choice 3. influence 4. manager 5. assistant 6. director 7. force 8. orientation
Übung 70: 1. into 2. in/on 3. on 4. for 5. in 6. from/about 7. at/in
Übung 71: 1. note 2. resemble 3. understand 4. begin 5. assume control 6. lift 7. launch 8. hire
Übung 72: 1. average 2. threatening 3. visit 4. mobile 5. out 6. investigate

Übung 73: 1. confirm 2. payment 3. forceful 4. counterpart 5. obvious 6. strange 7. put forward 8. profitable 9. costs
Übung 74: 1. inquiring 2. toes 3. passed 4. driven 5. turn 6. off 7. shortcut 8. mobile
Übung 75: 1. - 2. ✔ 3. ✔ 4. ✔ 5. - 6. - 7. ✔
Übung 76: 1. I have lived here for ten years. 2. She has gone to Moscow. 3. David Blood has been a detective for several years. 4. They have not given a thought to the next project. 5. We have tried everything! 6. Your tickets have just arrived. 7. Have you ever been to the headquarters?
Übung 77: 1. intruder 2. amused 3. answer 4. pursuit 5. pointed out 6. fruitless 7. deceptive
Übung 78: 1. Petrol prices are raised and lowered by the oil companies. 2. The car was driven recklessly (by Flowers). 3. The office was destroyed by the intruder. 4. The decision to invest in the struggling company was made six months ago. 5. Red and white wine is produced in Chile. 6. The good quality of German automobiles is recognised.
Übung 79: 1. How much 2. Why/When 3. Where 4. Which 5. When 6. How many/Which
Übung 80: 1. in 2. for 3. into 4. to 5. of 6. of 7. for
Übung 81: 1. excuse 2. command 3. repeat 4. colleague 5. assure 6. phony
Übung 82: 1. - 2. ✔ 3. - 4. - 5. ✔ 6. ✔
Übung 83: 1. c 2. a 3. b 4. b 5. a
Übung 84: 1. silence 2. moment 3. pieces 4. hung up 5. report 6. equipment 7. authorise
Übung 85: 1. circuitous 2. general 3. prohibit 4. cautious 5. suppress 6. produce 7. plummet
Übung 86: 1. She asks for a pay rise. 2. He seems to dislike telephones. 3. No, he is not. 4. He or she is known as a loss adjuster. 5. It is also known as a monitor. 6. He wants to look at Beyond 2050's financial records.
Übung 87: 1. surpize/surprise 2. respunded/responded 3. employers/employees 4. recrooting/recruiting 5. lead/led 6. familar/familiar 7. colleges/colleagues 8. invoved/involved
Übung 88: 1. control 2. statement 3. fees 4. research 5. sheets 6. options
Übung 89: 1. unlikely 2. value 3. subject 4. coordinate 5. present 6. involve 7. office 8. efforts 9. thereafter
Übung 90: 1. ✔ 2. - 3. ✔ 4. ✔ 5. - 6. ✔ 7. ✔
Übung 91: 1. work force 2. chief executive officer 3. middle management 4. senior management 5. board of directors 6. chief information officer
Übung 92: 1. at/of 2. of 3. of 4. on 5. of 6. if 7. in 8. to

Übung 93: 1. vortäuschen 2. Ringen 3. Sporthalle 4. Bibliothek 5. Betrug 6. trainieren
Übung 94: 1. freak 2. intention 3. mad 4. enhance 5. changling 6. particle
Übung 95: 1. described 2. respective 3. discussed 4. instalment 5. reported 6. found 7. funded 8. discovered 9. brought
Übung 96: 1. the 2. a 3. – 4. – 5. the 6. – 7. a
Übung 97: 1. stood 2. winked 3. could 4. got 5. brings 6. is/'s 7. is/'s
Übung 98: 1. - 2. ✔ 3. - 4. ✔ 5. - 6. - 7. ✔ 8. - 9. ✔ 10. ✔
Übung 99: 1. - 2. ✔ 3. - 4. ✔ 5. - 6. ✔ 7. ✔
Übung 100: 1. connection 2. circulate 3. recoup 4. institution 5. statement 6. call for 7. distributor

Lösungen Abschlusstest

Übung 1: 1. post 2. intervention 3. secretary 4. limitless 5. assure 6. report 7. income
Übung 2: 1. book 2. reliance 3. raising 4. fluctuations 5. discredit 6. frozen 7. enquiring 8. secured
Übung 3: 1. investment 2. bonus 3. entry 4. mentioned 5. turn 6. subject
Übung 4: 1. flourishing 2. skyrocket 3. suitable 4. turnover 5. engagement 6. employees 7. strange 8. lucrative
Übung 5: 1. Sally Fielding was much more than a secretary. 2. Detectives are hired to retrieve missing persons. 3. Have you finished the monthly report? 4. A solicitor is a member of the legal profession. 5. Blood asked the young man to escort him to the crime scene. 6. I'm no longer personal assistant at First Sea. 7. Get whatever information you can from him, okay?
Übung 6: 1. in 2. of 3. on 4. in 5. into 6. in 7. from 8. for 9. at/in
Übung 7: 1. receive mails 2. personnel manager 3. balance sheet 4. senior management 5. financial records 6. coordinate efforts 7. personal property 8. customer orientation 9. attend meetings
Übung 8: 1. on business 2. investigation 3. financial assets 4. convince/persuade 5. deliver 6. subject line 7. urgent(ly) 8. briefcase 9. participate 10. visitor's car park/parking lot
Übung 9: 1. She said she was very tired. 2. They said it had been a very interesting day. 3. She said she was always talking to herself. 4. He said they would be at the meeting on time. 5. She asked if I/he/she had got any money. 6. She suggested going to the Indian restaurant. 7. He said he could not change the appointment. 8. He said he had worked twelve hours the day before.